LANDS OF
THE THUNDERBOLT
SIKHIM, CHUMBI & BHUTAN

LANDS OF THE THUNDERBOLT
SIKHIM, CHUMBI & BHUTAN

BY THE
EARL OF RONALDSHAY
P.C., G.C.S.I., G.C.I.E.

HON, D. LITT, CALCUTTA; HON. D.L. DACCA
PRESIDENT OF THE ROYAL GEOGRAPHICAL SOCIETY
AUTHOR OF
'SPORT AND POLITICS UNDER AN EASTERN SKY'; 'ON THE OUTSKIRTS OF EMPIRE IN ASIA'; 'A WANDERING STUDENT IN THE FAR EAST,' AND 'AN EASTERN MISCELLANY'

GYAN

Published by

Gyan Publishing House
5, Ansari Road
Daryaganj, New Delhi-110002
Phone: 011-47034999, 9811692060
E-mail: books@gyanbooks.com

Distribution Network
gyanbooks.com
India, USA, Canada, UK, Australia, France

ISBN : 978-81-212-2359-1 (PB)
First Published, 1923

2nd Impression 2021

Printed at: Gyan Press, Delhi.

Lands of The Thunderbolt Sikhim, Chumbi & Bhutan
Author: Earl of Ronaldshay

LANDS OF THE THUNDERBOLT

SIKHIM, CHUMBI & BHUTAN

BY THE

EARL OF RONALDSHAY

P.C., G.C.S.I., G.C.I.E.

HON. D.LITT. CALCUTTA; HON. D.L. DACCA
PRESIDENT OF THE ROYAL GEOGRAPHICAL SOCIETY
AUTHOR OF
'SPORT AND POLITICS UNDER AN EASTERN SKY'; 'ON THE OUTSKIRTS OF EMPIRE IN ASIA'; 'A WANDERING STUDENT IN THE FAR EAST,' 'AN EASTERN MISCELLANY' AND 'INDIA A BIRD'S-EYE VIEW'

CONSTABLE AND COMPANY LIMITED
LONDON

Frontispiece.

THE SIKHIM WOODLAND

"The enchanted forest of one's childhood's dreams."

PREFACE

SOME explanation of the title which I have given to this volume is, perhaps, called for. The countries described are situated in the Eastern Himalayas on the northern borders of Bengal. They contain some of the most impressive mountain scenery in the world; and if their interest lay solely in their physical characteristics, they would be worthy of the homage of the most blasé traveller. Of Sikhim—the scene of the greater part of the excursions described in these pages—it has been said that it is probably the most mountainous country in the world; that within its small compass—it has an area of less than 3000 square miles—it rises in a tumult of ranges from 700 to 28,000 feet; that in a two hours' scramble one can descend from Alpine gentians to tropical bamboos; that the higher altitudes are ice and rock, the lower a wilderness of forest ridges and precipitous gorges, with seldom a level space and barely room for a footpath by the side of their torrent beds.[1]

But the interest of these countries by no

[1] Mr. W. H. Buchan in *Blackwood's Magazine* for April 1912.

means lies solely in their scenery, magnificent though it is. They possess also an unusual human interest by reason of the curious lines on which the thought of their people has developed, and of the strange customs and practices to which that thought has given rise. The peculiar bent of their minds has been produced by the meeting of two fundamentally opposed ideas concerning the nature of things which, instead of rebounding when they met, coalesced. Those ideas were rationalism on the one hand and superstition on the other. The former was represented by the metaphysics of early Buddhism; the latter by the demonolatry which, under the name of Bön-pa, passed for religion in primitive Tibet. It is true that the former had already undergone large changes as a result of contact with thought akin to that of the latter, before ever it penetrated the mountain regions; but the process of coalescence was completed after it had done so, and it is only in these countries that the thought and practice which are the products of this process have survived.

The man who more than any other was responsible for this paradoxical combination of ideas was a Buddhist missionary known in India as Guru Padma Sambhava, and in Tibet as Guru Rimpoché. The story of his mission, during which were laid the foundations of the elaborately organised religion to which the term *lamaism* is usually applied, is told hereafter. He became a power in the land, and one of the chief emblems of his might was the *vajrah,* or symbol of the thunderbolt of Indra. In Tibet the word *vajrah* became *dorjé,* and as time went on it became one of the most common of all the emblems associated with priestly power. It is almost always to be found among the objects on the altars in the temples. It is an essential object on the tables of the three priestly office-bearers whose duty it is to officiate at the temple services. The abbot or spiritual head of a monastery bears the title of Dorjé-lopon, "the wielder of the thunderbolt or sceptre." In Bhutan the title of the spiritual head of the country, known to the outside world as Dharma Raja, is Druk Gye-po, the meaning of which is the "Thunder king," that is to say, the king of the Drukpa or Thunderer sect of Buddhists; and his motto, engraved in the centre of his official seal, is *Bdag Druk Yin,* signifying "I am the Thunderer." And finally, Darjeeling, the name of the famous hill-station which was the starting-point of all the expeditions which form the subject matter of the following pages, is commonly said to be a corruption of Dorjé-ling, "the place of the thunderbolt," the name of a monastery which once stood on a well-known eminence in the modern town, now known as Observatory Hill. In the interests of historical accuracy I should, perhaps, add that I believe the commonly accepted explanation to be incorrect. A derivation seldom heard, but which I have the best of grounds for believing to be correct, is that which attributes the word Dorjé in the first half of Darjeeling to the name of a lama, Dorjé-rinzing, who founded the monastery which once stood on Observatory Hill. The shrine was subsequently removed to the Bhutia Basti, where it remains to this day; but the former site retained the name of "the place of Dorjé lama."

It is, however, immaterial to my present theme whether the true derivation is from "the place of the thunderbolt" or "the place of the lama named thunderbolt." Either theory bears witness to the fact that in lands in which symbols are at a premium the thunderbolt takes a prominent place. And in any flag or coat-of-arms designed for lamaism, in accordance with the traditions of heraldry, it would most assuredly appear as a conspicuous object. So much in explanation of the title.

The volume has been conceived as part of a larger whole which is designed to give some idea, not merely of the physical characteristics of the Indian empire, but of those subtler differences between East and West which are to be found in the thought and attitude towards life of its peoples. And from this point of view it is incomplete apart from its companion volumes. From a narrower point of view it may be regarded as self-contained. That is to say, viewed simply as a narrative of travel in somewhat out-of-the-way countries of great natural charm, and among people whose strange characteristics give them an unusual interest, it is complete in itself and is intelligible without reference to either of its companion volumes.

It has become almost a convention that a preface to a volume of this kind should conclude with the author's acknowledgements to a variety of persons for various services. Where I have been indebted to others for information or for opinions, I have acknowledged my indebtedness in the text. Such acknowledgement as I feel to be appropriate to this preface I prefer to make in the form of a dedication. I dedicate this volume (without permission) to the Elder, the Cavalry Officer, and the Sardar Bahadur, the almost constant and altogether delightful companions of the rambles of which these pages are the record.

But one word more in explanation of the invocation with which this volume opens. According to an ancient legend a request went forth from the famous University of Nalanda to the great Buddhist masters throughout India, from the mountains of Kashmir to the palm groves of Ceylon, that they should compete in composing a hymn in praise of Manjusri, the god of Wisdom. Five hundred learned teachers responded to the invitation; and when the five hundred hymns were examined it was found that they were identical, differing not by so much as a single word: an interesting parallel, it may be observed, with the case of the seventy-two Jews who, according to an ancient tradition, confined in separate cells, produced the seventy-two identical Greek versions of the Hebrew scriptures which came to be known as the Septuagint.

The obvious explanation of this apparent miracle was accepted, namely, that the five hundred composers had each and every one served but as the mouthpiece of Manjusri himself. Hence the vogue which this celebrated hymn enjoys to this day. For the translation I am indebted, with the exception of a few verbal alterations which I have ventured to make, to an erudite scholar of Sikhim, Kazi Dawa Samdup.

I should, perhaps, add *pro forma* that the illustrations are from photographs taken by myself.

RONALDSHAY.

January 1923.

CONTENTS

CHAPTER IX

CHAPTER X

CHAPTER XI

CHAPTER XII

CHAPTER XIII

CHAPTER XIV

CHAPTER XV

CHAPTER XVI

CHAPTER XVII

CHAPTER XVIII

CHAPTER XIX

CHAPTER XX

CHAPTER XXI

CHAPTER XXII

CHAPTER XXIII

ILLUSTRATIONS

HYMN TO MANJUSRI

Obeisance to the Divine Protecting Lord and Teacher Manjusri,
Whose Wisdom shineth forth gloriously, free from the two-fold mental gloom—like the sun free from clouds,
Bearing the sacred volume against his heart to symbolise His perfect knowledge of all Truth in its very reality.
Regarding those who are still in the captivity of the ocean of existence, enveloped in ignorance and its attendant suffering,
As a mother does her only son, and calling on them with his divinely sweet voice possessing the sixty vocal perfections,
The deep thrilling and thunder-like resonance of which arouses them from the deep sleep of ignorance and frees them from the fetters of Karma,
Bearing the Sword of Wisdom for cutting the weeds of suffering and lighting up the gloom of ignorance.
Pure from all Eternity, endowed with the divine attributes of those who have passed beyond the ten degrees of Perfections, O, Thou, chief amongst royal princes,
O, Thou, dispeller of the gloom of my heart, adorned with the hundred and twelve beautifying ornaments, obeisance to Thee.

Let the radiance and glory of thy Wisdom, O, Loving One,
Dispel the sloth and gloom of my heart.
Graciously bestow on me the light of courage and intellect,
That I may understand the sacred words and scriptures aright.

CHAPTER I

THE COMING OF SUMMER

WINTER in Bengal is short-lived. It would scarcely be recognised by the denizen of a temperate clime as winter at all. The landscape is studded with green trees. A warm sun shines daily from a cloudless sky. The mean temperature varies from 65° in January, when it is at its lowest, to 86° in May and June. And by the month of February Dame Nature is busy with her annual spring-cleaning. She plies her duster and broom vigorously among the trees, brushing off dead leaves which linger on after the new foliage has appeared and scattering them broadcast over the ground. For this reason spring is the nearest approach to an English autumn of which Bengal is capable.

But Dame Nature is not content with a mere superficial dusting. Donning her spring garments she takes up her palette and brush and she proves herself a wonderful artist. Bougainvilias and bauhiniyas she paints purple and mauve. She is lavish, too, with varying shades of yellow; but her most brilliant achievements are in full-blooded tints ranging from crimson to scarlet. Early in February she is at work on the cotton tree. She makes a clean sweep of the leaves, and in their place covers the spreading branches with large blossoms of vivid red the brilliance of whose colouring is accentuated by the absence of foliage which she has arranged. And scarcely has she started unfolding the blossoms on the cotton tree when she turns her attention to its rival, the palash or "flame of the forest," which she causes to burst into glorious flower. To the scarlet of its great clusters of flowers she adds a touch of ruddy gold, taking her idea, one may suppose, from the success which she has achieved in blending those colours beneath the rind of the blood orange. Her work, as always, is a wonderful harmony; and if the flower of the cotton tree seems to have borrowed its hue from the burning flush of the sky at sunset, the flame of the forest seems equally to reflect the burnished gold of a resplendent dawn.

In the meanwhile other influences are at work. About the time that she starts painting the forest, the wind veers round towards the south, rapidly losing all pretence of sharpness, and by March is blowing steadily from that direction. The maximum shade temperature creeps up to 90° F., and during March and April jumps frequently to over 100° F. The mean temperature during March climbs from 76° F. to 84° F., and by the end of the month it is for only a brief period during the twenty-four hours that the mercury drops a degree or two below 75° F. If summer has not yet come, winter at least has gone.

The man from Central and Northern India

accustomed to the stark aridity of his own country marvels at the wide diffusion of green; and mindful of the scorching temperatures of the lands from which he hails, where it is nothing unusual for the thermometer to register 120° in the shade, is apt to scoff at the comparative mildness of Bengal. He does not appreciate the significance of an atmospheric humidity which for a brief period only at the driest time of the year—April to May—falls below an average of 80 per cent, and which even at such times at any moment may—and, in fact, frequently does—rise above 90 per cent.

It is this burden of moisture that gives to the land its wonderful viridity, with its deceptive appearance of freshness. Its woods, so attractive to look at, become the haunts of brazen-tongued birds that punctuate the heavy hours during the heat of the day with their monotonous and exasperating cries. The too-well-named coppersmith hammers away on his single metallic note, and the brain-fever bird asks an eternal question in maddening ascending crescendo. And beyond the delusive shade of the trees the sun casts a fierce glare despite the abundance of green.

During these months the wind blowing from the Bay of Bengal passes like a warm breath across the land and piles itself up against the mountains in the far north. This process is not carried on without interruption. There are moments when it seems to be hurled back on its track, causing violent storms known familiarly as nor'-westers. The drowsy stillness of the afternoon is suddenly broken. There is a rustle and uneasy stirring among the trees. A cloud of dust scurries across the plain, and the storm sweeps down, driven madly along on a gale of wind. For a time the whole atmosphere is in a state of wild disturbance. Inky clouds rumbling ominously, and spitting jagged darts of flame, pour forth a deluge of water and then pass on again. The wind dies away and the rain ceases. For a short time there is a wonderful clearness in the air, and a fragrant smell rises from the ground. But these things are of short duration. The air becomes rapidly warm again and heavy with moisture which it drinks up from the saturated soil, and in the morning the sun burns and smites fiercely once more as if no storm had been.

In April, as if tired of so much fiery decoration, Dame Nature is at work again sweeping the red blossoms completely from the cotton tree and replacing them with a coating of fresh green. But she is far too great an artist not to appreciate the appropriateness of such colouring to the burning heat of the season which is rapidly approaching, and before long under her deft fingers the Gold Mohur flames fiercely into flower. One has little hesitation in proclaiming this to be her masterpiece. There is nothing that can surpass it in wealth of blossom or in richness of hue. And as if conscious of having reached the zenith of her fame she casts aside her palette and brush; and one becomes conscious that in place of the garment of spring she has almost imperceptibly changed into the hot and heavy cloak of summer.

Whatever opinion a man may hold of the agreeableness or otherwise of a Bengal spring, there can be no two opinions of the long and burdensome days of a Bengal summer. Before the sun has climbed far on its daily path one shuts up one's house, closing doors and windows against the entrance of the hot suffocating air. One labours grimly at one's desk, curbing one's irritation as one's papers scatter beneath the stirring of the close air caused by the electric fan. As one pants and perspires one thinks longingly of the cool breezes of the distant hills. And sooner or later, if one is free to do so, one follows in the flesh the nimbler flight of one's errant thoughts.

CHAPTER II

ACROSS THE PLAINS

A FAMOUS master of dialectic once found it necessary to point out that in all discussion it was reasonable to postulate, on the part of the parties to a controversy, a knowledge of such elementary factors in the case as might be regarded as being axiomatic. "If, for example," he explained, "I describe the Fen country of the Eastern Counties of England as a flat country, I take it for granted that those to whom I address my observation, understand that the statement is subject to such qualification as is due to the fact of the earth being round."

Subject to the same qualification it may be said with perfect truth that for thousands of square miles the Bengal landscape spreads itself in flat monotony to the farthest limits of sight. A man who had lived in the deltaic tracts of Bengal all his life could not possibly know the meaning of the word mountain, except by means of what the logicians call "derivative knowledge." It is true that the plain is an inclined one, but the inclination is so slight as to be almost negligible. Calcutta, which is distant eighty-six miles from the sea, is about twenty feet above mean sea-level, and during a journey of over three hundred miles north from the capital to Siliguri one rises less than four hundred feet.

It is difficult to discover in these three hundred miles any feature which is of assistance in painting the landscape upon one's memory. There is neither hill nor rock, nor, indeed, so much as a stone, to dispute the unchallenged ascendancy of the rich alluvial soil. During the early summer the whole land would present to the eye an unruffled expanse of burnt sienna, were it not for an abundance of semi-tropical vegetation spread in irregular patches all over the scene. Bamboos, palms, plantains, mangoes, banyans, and a host of other trees, clad sumptuously with foliage and in some cases with flowers, flourish in dense clumps—the product of a rich soil and of a languorous and vapour-laden atmosphere.

As in the case of almost all rural scenes in India, the predominant note is one of untidiness. One is left with the impression that here Nature is still rudely defiant of the efforts of man. His handiwork is apparent certainly—one sees it in the drab fields that presently will bring forth an abundance of rice, and in the picturesque collections of fragile and unambitious buildings in which he dwells. But all the time one knows that he is there on sufferance. The whole landscape is much nearer to Nature—primeval, untutored Nature—than an agricultural landscape in Europe, for example. The exuberant vitality of the great life principle of Nature lurks amongst the dense thickets, ever responsive to the creative caress of the warm moisture-laden air. The

Great Mother waits only the moment of man's departure to spread over the earth a dense coverlet of riotous vegetation. And, in fact, on all sides of one this is actually happening. Villages deserted for one cause or another—an epidemic of disease or the shifting of a water-course—are swallowed up by the jungle, and the place thereof knows them no more. Buildings of brick and stone are equally powerless before the inexorable advance of the jungle, which, if permitted to do so, sooner or later closes in upon them and brings about their dissolution. There are many parts of Bengal where it is no uncommon thing to see trees of appreciable size growing upon the almost perpendicular brick spires of the temples. On one occasion I received a petition from the congregation of a mosque in Chittagong for the restoration of the building, it being stated by the petitioners that the floor was sinking and the building tumbling down, roots of plants having penetrated deep into the walls. But the most amazing example of the power of the Bengal jungle that I have come across is provided by the ruins on the outskirts of the ancient city of Murshidabad. Here the forest has completely swallowed up the great artillery park of the famous line of the Nawabs who ruled Bengal from that city. A solitary relic of the past gives indication of the site once bristling with the guns of this powerful line of oriental rulers. It consists of a huge cannon seventeen feet six inches in length and five feet in circumference, weighing, according to an ancient inscription, seven and a half tons. The remarkable thing about it is that it hangs suspended horizontally some feet above the ground, embedded in the *trunk* of a pipal tree which has wrapped itself about it and now holds it aloft in an iron grip. With such examples before one's eyes one realises why it is that there are few historic buildings in Bengal.

There is undoubtedly a curious fascination attaching to these vast spaces with their chequered green surfaces. To the people inhabiting them they make an immense appeal. For the great Bengali poet of the nineteenth and twentieth centuries there is no land that can compare with them for natural beauty. These limitless level spaces fill him with an exuberant joy. He writes with a love amounting to passion of "the unobstructed sky filled to the brim, like an amethyst cup, with the descending twilight and peace of the evening," and he speaks with reverential wonder of "the golden skirt of the still, silent noonday" spreading over the whole immensity of the landscape "without let or hindrance."[1]

But it is not of these lands of great spaces that I am now about to write. The chapters that follow rest upon a very different background—a crumpled world of towering mountains, the very antithesis of the unbroken surfaces of the Bengal plains. And these few sentences have been written for the reason that there is one beauty of the plains and another of the mountains, and that the beauty of the one provides just the foil required to enhance the beauty of the other.

[1] Letter from Sir Rabindranath Tagore to a friend dated September the 22nd, 1894.

CHAPTER III

A GREAT ASCENT

THE traveller from Calcutta steams into Siliguri in the early morning, and if he is not too weary to exercise his powers of observation he will at once find indications that he stands upon the threshold of a different world. The monotony of the country through which he has been passing is interrupted. It is interrupted most palpably by the appearance of a new type of humanity. Men and women with strongly marked Mongolian features and wearing more ample and more picturesque garments make their appearance upon the scene. But there are other things less pronounced, perhaps, but nevertheless perceptible, whose cumulative effect is to arouse an expectation of change. Siliguri is palpably a place of meeting. Rolling stock of two distinct types stand in rows on the railway sidings. Large sheds with corrugated iron roofs overshadow the usual mat and thatch house of the Bengali peasant, suggesting the temporary storage of produce in process of transportation from one region to another. Collections of outspanned bullock-carts add to the impression. The discovery that here the metre gauge system ends and the two-foot gauge of the Darjeeling-Himalayan railway begins, confirms all that these things hint at.

Presently the morning haze which dims the horizon to the north assumes vague forms. It seems to be crystallising in masses of dark and blurred outline. Interest, dulled by the heat and jaded by the monotony of the past, revives. One steps into a railway carriage which might easily be mistaken for a toy, and the whimsical idea seizes hold of one that one has stumbled accidentally into Lilliput. With a noisy fuss out of all proportion to its size the engine gives a jerk—and starts. The buildings of Siliguri, iron-roofed sheds, railway workshops of brick, stacks of timber, and here and there a one-storied bungalow resting in mid-air upon an under-structure of substantial piles, straggle along on either side of the miniature track until they are brought to an abrupt standstill by the broad bed of the Mahanadi river. As one puffs along at something over ten miles an hour, the amorphous shapes in front of one take on clearer definition, and before long stand out as giant tree-clad spurs of the outer Himalaya. Cultivation merges into forest of densely packed timber trees festooned with creepers.

Six miles from Siliguri we pull up at Sukna, a small station buried in forest at the foot of a wall of mountains. We have risen a hundred and thirty feet in the six miles without noticing it; from Sukna onwards, we are climbing stertorously for forty miles, in the course of which we scale close upon seven thousand feet of rugged mountain. No special mechanical device such as a rack is employed—unless, indeed, one can so describe the squat and stolid hill-man who sits perched over the forward buffers of the engine and scatters sand on the rails when the wheels of the engine lose their grip of the metals and race, with the noise of a giant spring running down when control has been removed. Sometimes we cross our own track after completing the circuit of a cone, at others we zigzag backwards and forwards; but always we climb at a steady gradient—so steady that if one embarks in a trolley at Ghum, the highest point on the line, the initial push supplies all the energy necessary to carry one to the bottom. I speak from personal knowledge when I say that to travel forty miles with no adventitious aid beyond that of one's own momentum is a novel and an agreeable experience.

As one climbs higher one passes into a clearer air, and looking down upon the plains from which one has come one perceives them soft and indistinct through an atmosphere saturated with moisture. One such glimpse is sufficient to explain the why and wherefore of many things—of mosquitoes and malaria, of prickly heat and irritability of temper, of certain plainly marked characteristics of the people inhabiting these soggy plains which may be summed up compendiously as inertia.

If one makes the journey at any time between the end of March and the beginning of November one is pretty certain to find oneself enveloped in mist or in rain before reaching one's destination. This is inevitable under the circumstances, for the colder air of the mountains can no longer retain the moisture with which the hot air of the plains is saturated, and condensation is bound to take place. The annual rainfall at Darjeeling is approximately 122 inches, and of this amount all but about 4½ inches falls between March and November.

Once over the outer range one finds oneself in a world as different from that which one has left behind in the morning as Scotland is from the Sahara. Darjeeling itself is completely walled off from the plains, for its buildings cling to the summit and flanks of a spur which juts out abruptly from the northern face of the outer range of mountains. The spur itself hangs suspended above the deep valley of the Rungeet river which flows at right angles to it, six thousand feet below. On the farther side of the river rise ranges of mountains in gigantic tiers, so that if one stands with one's back to the main axis of the outer range one is faced by a vast amphitheatre of mountains filling in the little state of Sikhim and lifting themselves up in the far distance from the lofty highlands of Tibet. The culminating point in this stupendous panorama is the mass of Kanchenjunga, which rises to a height of over 28,000 feet above sea-level and 21,000 feet above one's own level as one observes it from Darjeeling.

The watershed of the main outer chain which is crossed on the journey to Darjeeling runs west for some distance and then curves northwards. A series of rivers flow down its northern and eastern slopes into the basin which is drained by the Rungeet. The latter river itself flows parallel to this range—that is to say, from its source in the great plexus of mountains leading up to Kanchenjunga it flows south until it strikes the elbow of the range, when it turns east past the Darjeeling spur until it empties itself into the Tista which carries the waters of Sikhim through a vast gap in the mountain system to the plains of Bengal. During its southward course it is joined by a network of rivers which have scoured deep valleys in the mountain system, reducing it to a chaotic tangle of peaks and spurs. To put it in another way. The outer range of the Himalayas rising abruptly from the plains of northern Bengal, is like the wall enclosing a vast natural amphitheatre in which lie the lovely mountains and valleys of Sikhim. And it is from the summit of this wall, consequently, that can be obtained the best bird's-eye view of that delightful country. The route along the watershed is, therefore, the obvious one for a preliminary survey.

Plate 2.

THE HIGHLANDS OF SIKHIM: MOUNT JANNU, THE EAGLE PEAK.

CHAPTER IV

THE RIM OF THE AMPHITHEATRE

OUR baggage packed and shouldered by the sturdy Bhutia women who obligingly undertake the duties of pack animals, nothing remained but to grasp our staves and set foot on the tortuous mountain path which we had decided to follow. An outstanding feature of the eastern Himalayas is the immense luxuriance and variety of their vegetation. Along the valley bottoms less than a thousand feet above sea-level tropical growths flourish. From this one may pass to the subtropical zone and on again through the temperate to an alpine region running up to the eternal snows themselves. The watershed of the range along which we were about to travel varies from eight to twelve thousand feet in height, and its wooded slopes, if I might believe the Elder who spoke with all the authority conferred by actual experience, would be studded with splendid specimens of different varieties of the great tree rhododendron which in April and May paints the forest scarlet, crimson, and yellow, and of the towering magnolia resplendent with its star-like blossoms of waxy white.

Throughout the first day we travelled sometimes on foot, sometimes on the stocky little ponies of the country, along the southern slopes of the range a little below the watershed, spending the night in a comfortable wooden bungalow at Jorepokri—" the two ponds "—rather more than twelve miles out from Darjeeling.

These southern slopes facing the steaming plains are clad with dense forest, the characteristics of which are peculiar; yet one finds oneself being gradually assailed with the curious sensation of having seen them before. The large timber trees throw out gnarled and many-forked branches. Trunk and branches alike are heavily festooned with clinging, beard-like moss and are much intertwined with sinuous, creeping growths. Among these sombre surroundings Nature, in so far as she expresses herself in sound at all, does so in harsh and monotonous tones. Vast numbers of tree frogs rasp out a raucous metallic buzz, while the birds pipe shrill and staccato notes. The whole effect is eerie, and with the realisation that this is so, memory suddenly flashes into consciousness. One is face to face with the enchanted forest of one's childhood's dreams—the home of sprites and witches pictured for us by the bizarre fancy of Hans Andersen and Grimm and by the skilful hands of Arthur Rackham and M. Edmund Dulac.

From Jorepokri the track runs to the populous village of Simāna-basti and then drops a thousand feet to a saddle in the range a short distance above the source of the Little Rungeet. From this point it rises steeply again for six miles to Tonglu, a bungalow prettily situated at an altitude of ten thousand feet.

Plate 3.

WOMEN OF THE HILLS.

" Sturdy Bhutia women who obligingly undertake the duties of pack animals."

The Elder is a man of weight, and the jobmaster in Darjeeling who dealt in Bhutia ponies was in the habit of reserving for his use a particular animal somewhat above the normal size. He was a good pony, but he was troubled with one failing, a certain weakness in that part of his anatomy which Dr. Johnson, out of sheer ignorance, as he subsequently admitted to an astonished questioner, defined as " the knee of a horse." He was, as the Sardar Bahadur put it, a devout creature who was always upon his knees. I was somewhat alarmed the first time I noticed him assuming an attitude of prayer at what seemed to me to be a particularly ill-chosen spot on a steep descent. But I became reassured upon observing the behaviour of the Elder. Did he pitch over the animal's head as I felt that I should have done ? Certainly not. Did he dismount as ninety-nine people out of a hundred would undoubtedly have done under similar circumstances ? Nothing of the sort. On the contrary, he adopted an attitude which can only be adequately described as one of masterly inactivity. Seated well back, his face suffused with an expression of detached unconcern, he waited patiently for his steed to rise. So far as he was concerned constant repetition had deprived the performance of the interest which it might once have possessed ; and after the first exhibition or two, these practices passed without comment from any of the party. It should be added that in adopting this attitude the Elder was invariably justified by the result. Sooner or later his steed did rise. On one occasion rider and pony went cheerfully through a bridge—one of those bridges that are not guaranteed by the D.P.W., *i.e.* the Department of Public Works, "to carry a load of more than five tons." But that is another story. I do not now remember how often he came with us, but I am certain that we all felt that we had lost a well-established member of our party when, as a result of what I feel constrained to characterise as the gratuitous intervention of the Society for the Prevention of Cruelty to Animals, he accompanied us no more.

From Tonglu to Sandakphu, 11,929 feet, a distance of fourteen miles, and thence to Phalut, 11,811 feet, a farther twelve miles, the forest through which we travelled did, indeed, contain splendid specimens of the rhododendron for which the Darjeeling and Sikhim Himalayas are famous. Of the thirty varieties which flourish at varying altitudes a number may easily be picked out in the course of this two days' march, ranging from the tall rough-barked *arborium*, which grows to a height of thirty feet, to the dwarf *lepidotum*, which seldom attains a stature of two feet and at high altitudes is usually much less. Between these two one notices *barbatum*, a large bush with smooth bark, which flowers in April ; *campanulatum*, a stunted variety with numerous slender stems springing upward from close to the ground, which flowers in June ; *Falconeri*, a fine tree with a large leaf coloured tawny on the lower side ; and *Hodgsoni*, a tree with a bark only less smooth than that of *barbatum*. Vying in beauty with rhododendrons are specimens of the splendid *Magnolia globosa*, its mass of white, star-like blossoms in the late spring standing out in sharp contrast upon its leafless branches.

On the summit of the range between Sandakphu and Phalut, one follows the boundary between British India and Nepal across open grass-covered spaces where the flora assumes an Alpine character. The little mauve *Primula peliolata*, which covers the banks in the forest, gives place to a flower resembling a cowslip in shape, but mauve in colour, the *Primula denticulata*, which grows in great quantity on the open grass-covered slopes. Blue and white anemones add a further touch of colour to the ground, and large patches of a grey everlasting, *anaphalis*, abound.

These outer ranges of the eastern Himalaya, as I have already stated, are only too often shrouded in mist ; and I have been and returned along the Sandakphu range without so much as catching a glimpse of the world beyond the ridge itself. But I recall one memorable occasion on which the veil was torn aside and the vast arc of the Himalaya was displayed in all its marvellous beauty. After nightfall the mist which had been thick all day cleared off and we could see far away to the south-east across an immeasurable abyss, the lights of Darjeeling gleaming like small yellow luminous dots upon an invisible background. The air was cold, and our hopes that daylight might dawn upon an atmosphere still clear of cloud were realised. From our point of vantage on the summit of the range we could gaze south over the low-lying plains of northern Bengal, and west, north, and east over an interminable tangle of mountains to the eternal snows.

The plains lay sleeping beneath a wonderful quilt of billowy white cloud. In the foreground of the mountain picture, too, tumbled masses of cloud rested lazily on the valley bottoms, while over and beyond these alternate layers of cloud and mountain ridge which stretched away from our feet, there rose in sublime grandeur, clear cut against a blue sky and ringing in the whole of the northern horizon, a continuous chain of snow-clad mountains.

There cannot be many spots on earth, standing upon which a man may say that he is gazing at one and the same moment upon three out of the four greatest mountains of the world. Phalut is one of them. Away to the west Mount Everest towers aloft, while close by a little to the north and forming part of the same group stands Makalu. Nearer the centre of the picture and closer to the observer rises the stupendous *massif* of Kanchenjunga. Mathematics is a coldly prosaic science, since it ignores qualities and takes account only of quantities, and is an intruder, therefore, in the world of aesthetics. It affords, however, the only convenient means of conveying an idea of comparative magnitudes, and for the benefit of those who have not had the advantage of seeing this superb panorama themselves, it is worth recording that the altitudes of the three peaks mentioned are 29,002 feet, 27,790 feet, and 28,146 feet respectively.

While I was still drinking in the beauty of the scene Nature started drawing her giant curtain across my view. Eddying shapes of mist blew smudgily across the world, and by

9 A.M. had blotted out mountain and valley for the day.

From Phalut one may cross into Sikhim by the shoulder of Mount Singalela, a steep grass-covered hill studded with numerous outcrops of rock, where British India, Nepal, and Sikhim meet, and thence drop precipitately some seven or eight thousand feet into the valley of the Kulhait river. The moment we entered Sikhim we received striking demonstration of the welcome which its people were prepared to give us. The warmest hospitality was, indeed, invariably shown to us whenever we travelled in the country, and it found outward expression in music and refreshment—each in kind peculiar to the country. On no occasion that I can recall during the numerous excursions which I made, did I ever visit a monastery or an important village without receiving this attention.

The Sikhim band varies in size and in the quality of its instruments. It always contains one or more drums carried on the back of one man and beaten lustily by another walking immediately behind him, as it moves in exiguous procession along the narrow mountain paths. It also contains strange wind instruments known as Nepali horns, and not infrequently an apparatus which produces the noise of the drone of a bagpipe. The Elder, who at times gives evidence of an imagination capable of perilous flights, on listening on one occasion to an animated performance on a particularly large array of these instruments, concluded that it was a special rendering of "Scotland for ever," given doubtless, as he put it, "out of courtesy to our nationality."

The one invariable beverage which was offered to us at all times and in all places was the national drink, a decoction of millet called *marwa*. The millet is treated somewhat elaborately with a view to its fermentation. When ready for consumption the fermented grain is placed in a vessel consisting of a section of bamboo known as a *chūnga*. Hot water is then poured into it and sucked up through a reed. The same chūnga of marwa may be replenished with hot water repeatedly until all virtue has gone out of it. The question whether or not this beverage was to be regarded as coming within the definition of a temperance drink, was unexpectedly settled one day in the course of the following conversation which took place as we sucked at our chūngas in a shady arbour, raised by the wayside by the head man of a neighbouring village for our entertainment.

The Elder. "How often can the same chūngaful of millet be replenished with water ?"

The Sardar Bahadur. "Oh, many times !"

The Elder. "And what is done with the millet when the chūnga is finished with ?"

The Sardar Bahadur. "It is given to the pigs." He looked at us reflectively and then after a pause added—"And the pigs get drunk too !"

The Elder attributed the use of the word "too" to an incomplete appreciation on the part of the Sardar Bahadur of the niceties of the English language.

The village of Dentam on the right bank of the Kulhait river, stands on the slope of a mountain the face of which is scored with series of beautifully constructed terraces on which the millet and other crops are grown. A day's journey from here brings one to Sanga Chelling, or "the place of secret spells," reputed to be one of the first monasteries built in Sikhim, and a little farther on to Pemiongchi, the most wealthy of all the Sikhim monasteries of the present day. Both are situated on spurs of the same heavily wooded ridge, which in its turn is surrounded by similar crests and spurs, each crowned with a similar building. On these picturesque but lonely heights the priesthood of the country has built its monasteries and temples; and here the curious traveller may see and study an interesting by-product of India's never-ending search after knowledge—of her immense and tireless effort to grasp the elusive WHY of all things. And here, consequently, one becomes aware that the interest and attraction of the Sikhim Himalayas are not confined to their incomparable natural beauty. When one encounters men and women industriously turning small metal cylinders packed with paper rolls of prayers, and so constructed that a comparatively gentle movement of the wrist causes them to revolve on rough wooden handles as on an axle, one's curiosity is naturally aroused.

An explanation of the object of this widespread practice, which at first sight appears chiefly remarkable for its patent futility, sets one speeding in imagination to the ancient deer park at Isipatana near Benares, where, two and a half millenniums ago, Siddartha Gautama, since known to the world as the Buddha, preached his first great sermon to a small band of wandering friars, and so—less literally than the hill-folk of to-day, but with far greater efficacy—first set in motion the wheel of the law. There is something which is in part humorous and in part pathetic in the devotion of so much time and energy to the actual mechanical turning of the wheel of the law; and since I am about to record my experiences of the curiously unorthodox form of Buddhism prevalent in Sikhim and Tibet under the name of Lamaism, I am oppressed with a sense of the necessity of prefacing what I have to say, by a brief description of the purer form of Buddhism from which the Tibetan offshoot has sprung. Hence the interpolation by way of parenthesis of some pages, concerned in part with history and in part with metaphysics, in a collection of unpretentious sketches of the people and countries which are limned in, in picturesque outline, in the background of any comprehensive landscape of Bengal.

Plate 4.

SETTING IN MOTION THE WHEEL OF THE LAW.

"Men and women industriously turning small metal cylinders . . .

CHAPTER V

HISTORY OR STORY ?

SIDDARTHA GAUTAMA, usually spoken of simply as Buddha, is unquestionably one of the outstanding figures of the world. The story of his life, depicting, as it does, a human soul awakened suddenly to the inexplicability of human existence, girding fiercely against the narrow limitations of human understanding and struggling desperately after an intelligible solution of the problems with which it is hedged around, is one which is profoundly affecting and constitutes a human document unsurpassed in interest in the annals of mankind.

Curiously enough, an attempt has been made to read into his life-history an Indian version of the ubiquitous solar myth; to assume in place of the actual incidents of an outstanding career a skilful weaving into the life of a very ordinary person of the threads of the almost universal allegory of the Sun-God. Such a theory is, surely, absurdly far-fetched—the outcome of the desire of a certain methodical type of mind to reduce every ancient expression of the religious impulses of mankind to the dead level of a common denominator; and I reject it utterly. For me the Buddha of story lived.

And why should he not have lived? Men with minds akin to his have existed in India in all ages and are to be found there at the present day—men who, thinking on the same lines as Buddha thought, experience the same impulses and act in very much the same way. In western lands Ramkrishna Paramahaṁsha, the saintly ascetic who dwelt in the temple at Dakineshwar on the outskirts of Calcutta, and who died only in the year 1886, would have been as unlooked for as Siddartha Gautama. But in India such men have at all times been numerous. When a young college student, Narendra Nath Dutt, sat at the feet of Ramkrishna and in due course, discarding the garments and pursuits of a conventional career, went forth as Swami Vivekenanda in quest of truth, he excited veneration but no surprise. These things are part and parcel of the life of India. At Belur Math, the headquarters of the Ramkrishna Mission on the banks of the Hughli, I met a young man with the shaven head and in the yellow robes of the order. He had come down from the *ashram* of Mayavati, a hermitage devoted to the study and practice of Advaita (monistic) Vedanta, situated on a remote hill-top in the Himalayas, where he was living an austere life as head of the *ashram*. He was an M.A. of the Calcutta University. Examples might be multiplied indefinitely.

It is no doubt true that the story of the life of Gautama, in so far as it is recorded in the Pali and Sanskrit texts at all, is largely mythical. It is interspersed with miraculous happenings and has been fitted into a mythological framework constructed at a later date to square with the ingenious but wholly fanciful hypotheses of the later Buddhist theologians. But to relegate the story to the realms of pure fiction on this account would be absurd. Amongst an illiterate people the most extravagant beliefs spring up like weeds around the lives of those who, for one reason or another, excite their interest and fire their imagination. I have myself witnessed such miracles in the making. The simplicity of the process is amazing and from some points of view distinctly disconcerting, for it necessarily stimulates scepticism and places a discount upon faith. It was glaringly in evidence in connection with the campaign or mission—it is difficult to decide which is the more appropriate word—inaugurated by a now famous figure, that of Mr.—known to the masses of India as Mahatma—Gandhi in the year 1920.

Regarded from one point of view his campaign, which came to be known by the title "non-violent non-coöperation," might be looked upon simply as a political campaign against the Government. His avowed object was the obtaining of *swaraj*, a term popularly interpreted as deliverance in a political sense, *i.e.* from alien rule, but in origin a Vedic term signifying rather deliverance in the sense in which that word has at all times been so widely employed in India by her philosophers and theologians. I do not pause here to discuss the matter further from this particular point of view. It is unlikely that the illiterate masses, over whom Mr. Gandhi obtained a quite remarkable influence, asked themselves what was the precise object which he had in view. To them he was MAHATMA —" a great soul "—indeed to many he was more, he was an *avatar*, that is to say, an incarnation of God. And in the case of the vast majority of those who so regarded him they did not think of asking questions, but gave him blind allegiance.

Here, then, was an outstanding figure making a powerful appeal to the imagination of illiterate man in the mass; and immediately stories of the miraculous, as surprising as any of those told of Gautama Buddha, were to be heard passing from mouth to mouth at the village markets, spreading with the inexplicable rapidity which has often been remarked on in the case of news in India.

In parts of Bengal he was regarded as an avatar of Vishnu. It was said that attempts by Government to imprison him had failed because before his touch locks gave way and prison gates flew open. A little later it was reported to me that a story was circulating among the lower classes in the neighbourhood of Calcutta that a bomb thrown at him by an emissary of Government had melted like snow as soon as it touched his person. It was, further, widely believed that he had the power commonly attributed to the yogis of old, of turning people to stone. In parts of Bihar and the United Provinces his photograph was worshipped regularly; and a writer in an Indian newspaper, after making inquiries among people engaged in many of the humbler walks in life, declared that nearly all attributed supernatural powers to the Mahatma, and even bore personal testimony to them. On one occasion, he was told, the Mahatma had brought a dead man back to life by simply uttering the word "*Jito*"—"Come to life."

These things, occurring as they did in the twentieth century, provide a study in human credulity of quite extraordinary interest, and from the point of view of both the psychologist and the historian of great value; and for this reason I add to the examples given above, which would otherwise be sufficient for the purpose of my argument.

Take, for example, the following case. The Mahatma was addressing a gathering of villagers in the province of Bihar. At the conclusion one man bolder than the rest ventured to dispute his contentions. What was the result? I tell the story substantially as it was reported in the columns of an Indian-owned newspaper, the *Bengalee*, of April the 7th, 1921. The man died and his body was covered by those present with a basket. The police officer sent from the neighbouring police station to inquire into the matter found the basket lying on the ground and asked what lay beneath it. He was informed that the thing which lay covered was "*haram*," that is, untouchable. On the basket being lifted, it was seen that the corpse which lay beneath it had been changed to that of a pig.

With the circulation of such stories the fame of the Mahatma was noised abroad, and his teaching and the miracles by which it was accompanied, were discussed wherever men gathered together. Thus certain of the people of the village of Khalilabad, while resting during the heat of the day in a neighbouring mango grove, spoke of the wondrous doings of which they had heard. And one amongst them wishing to put matters to the test rose up and exclaimed, "If the doctrine of Mahatmaji is right and true, let a ripe mango drop from the trees!" And lo! to their utter astonishment a mango suddenly blossomed forth upon one of the branches and ripening miraculously, fell into the midst of the company. This story was told in the columns of the *Leader*, an Indian-owned newspaper of Allahabad, by Mr. Muhammad Ishak Khan of Basti, who added that he had heard it from one of those who had himself witnessed the miracle.

One more example. At the conclusion of a meeting addressed by Gandhi and some of his supporters in the district of Gaya, contributions were invited to the Swaraj fund. Some hesitation was displayed, and a man of the name of Kailash not only refused to subscribe to the fund but scoffed openly at the non-coöperation programme. It seems, however, that on hearing of the supernatural powers with which the Mahatma was credited, he became apprehensive and invited a number of Brahmans of the neighbourhood to a banquet, for the purpose of acquiring favour and securing their protection. The subsequent events were told by a man of the village in which they were alleged to have occurred, in the course of a speech in Calcutta on April the 16th, 1921. The Brahmans came as bidden, but were powerless against the might of the Mahatma. For when the covers were removed from the dishes the food provided by Kailash was found to have been turned into blood.

Finally, let me record a pathetic example of the unquestioning faith of the masses in the supernatural powers of the Mahatma—faith even unto death. It occurred not in the first flush of enthusiasm evoked by his campaign, but in February 1922, some three years after his first definite challenge to Government. A party of police in the course of their duty had effected certain arrests in the Jalpaiguri district of Bengal. On leaving they were attacked by a mob of villagers wearing the simple and inexpensive head-dress of white cotton prescribed by the Mahatma and known as the Gandhi cap. Repeated warnings by the police failed to stay the onslaught, and eventually it became necessary to open fire. The few casualties which resulted produced consternation in the ranks of the attackers, who immediately retired, leaving the police to continue on their way without further molestation. The explanation of the action of the villagers was forthcoming the next day when, in the course of an inquiry which was held, they stated that they had been told, and had believed, that so long as they were wearing the Gandhi cap, no bullet or shot had power to injure them.

Let it be remembered that these things were told and widely believed of a prominent public man during his lifetime, and that, too, in the twentieth century A.D. Need we feel surprised, then, if we read of Buddha that coming to the river Ganges at the time of high flood he, "as instantaneously as a strong man would stretch forth his arm or draw it back again when he had stretched it forth, vanished from this side of the river and stood on the farther bank with a company of the brethren"?[1] Or when we are told by a Chinese pilgrim visiting the spot a thousand years after the death of Buddha, how the latter miraculously defeated the plot of one Srigupta to bring about his death? The story is worth repeating for the purpose of bringing out the similarity between the miracles told of a preacher who lived five hundred years before Christ and those told of a preacher in the same locality—for most of the miracles which I have related of Gandhi took place in or near the ancient kingdom of Magadah—nearly two thousand years after Christ.

The episode is related as occurring at the city of Rajagriha, at that time the capital of Bimbisara, king of Magadah. At a certain spot we are told "there is a very deep ditch by the side of which is built a *stupa.* This is the spot where Srigupta wished to destroy Buddha by means of fire concealed in the ditch." After describing Srigupta's preparations, Hiuen Tsiang proceeds as follows: "Then all the people in the town knowing the evil and destructive design of Srigupta against the Lord of the World entreated Buddha not to go to the house. The Lord said, 'Be not distressed; the body of Tathāgata cannot be hurt by such means as these.' He therefore accepted the invitation and went. When his foot trod on the threshold of the door, the fire in the pit became a tank of pure water with lotus flowers on its surface."[2]

[1] *The Book of the Great Decease*, translated by T. W. and C. A. F. Rhys Davids.

[2] *Buddhist Records of the Western World*, Book IX.

Compared with some of the miracles attributed to Gandhi, the stories of levitation and similar feats told of the disciples of Buddha need excite little wonder. The well-known story, for example, of the performances, at the request of Buddha, of the Venerable Sagata, when the former was desirous of attracting the attention of a great assembly of the head men of the villages of Magadah, may very well have been concocted for the same purpose as the story of Gandhi and Kailash's feast to the Brahmans, namely, that of impressing upon the people the greatness of the preacher. On receiving the orders of Buddha the Venerable Sagata "rose up into the air and walked on high in the atmosphere, descended, sat down, emitted smoke and flames and vanished." Having done all these things he reappeared, and bowing down before Buddha exclaimed, "My Master, Sire, is the Exalted One; I am his disciple." Whereupon, we are told, the eighty thousand village Elders thought—"truly this is glorious, truly it is wonderful: if the disciple is so exceedingly mighty, what will the Master be?"

It is, indeed, far less surprising to find story thus intertwined with history in the case of Gautama than it is in the case of Gandhi, for the Buddhist scriptures were not committed to writing until long after the days of Buddha. It is true that it is stated by the Chinese pilgrims who visited India early in the seventh century A.D., that the three pitakas comprising what is usually known as the orthodox Canon, were inscribed upon the leaf of the *peito* (the palm leaf) and widely distributed at the first council alleged to have been held immediately after the death of Buddha. The Chinese pilgrims, however, were writing a thousand years after the event, and little confidence can be placed in statements of the kind. Moreover, it was not customary to employ writing for such purposes in those early centuries. The literature of the day was mnemonic and was handed down orally, and there is far more evidence in support of the very definite statement which occurs in the *Mahavamsa*—the great chronicle of Ceylon—that the committal of the sacred books to writing took place at a much later date. "The text of the three *pitakas*," we read, "and the *atthakatha* (commentary) thereon did the most wise *bhikkus* hand down in former times orally; but since they saw that the people were falling away the *bhikkus* came together, and in order that the true doctrine might endure, they wrote them down in books."[1] This statement occurs at the end of the account of the reign of King Vattagamani-Abhaya, whose probable date is 29–17 B.C. If, then, the obvious inference that the scriptures were committed to writing during his reign is correct, we have a period of more than four hundred and fifty years, marked, as we know, by heresies and schisms, intervening between the occurrence of the events and their committal to writing. The *Mahavamsa* was probably composed by Mahanama at the beginning of the sixth century A.D.; but in the opinion of scholars of repute its author had earlier manuscripts to work on, and in this matter all the arguments are on

[1] *Mahavamsa*, ch. xxxiii., verses 100 and 101. Professor Geiger's version.

Plate 5.

A HIGH PRIEST OF LAMAISM, THE ABBOT OF NAMCHI.

the side of "the great chronicle" and against the casual remark of the Chinese pilgrims.

I have written at what may be thought to be unnecessary length, in explanation of the mixture of fact and fiction in the narratives which have come down to us of the life and times of Gautama, the Buddha. I have done so not merely for the sake of showing that these particular narratives, interspersed though they are with miraculous happenings, may nevertheless contain much that is historically true; but also because of the remarkable illustration provided by events which I happened to be in a position to keep under close personal observation of the converse, namely, of the ease with which, in the case of an illiterate people, events which are historically true may become obscured even at the time of their occurrence by an amazing incrustation of pure fiction.

With this object-lesson before one it would be rash indeed to affirm of any particular episode in the life of Gautama, as it has been handed down to us in the Pali and later Sanskrit texts, that it is historically true. It is, however, quite possible to gather together the underlying threads of the story which wear a reasonable appearance of being a record of actual facts. And this is all that is necessary for my purpose. Let me endeavour, then, to give a brief sketch of his life as it probably was.

CHAPTER VI

THE LIFE OF BUDDHA

SIDDARTHA GAUTAMA was born in the year 563 B.C. of aristocratic and wealthy parents of the Sakya tribe, living at Kapilavastu near the Himalayan foot-hills in what is now known as the Nepal terai, about one hundred miles north-east of Benares. Particular care seems to have been taken by his parents to prevent him from coming into contact with the seamy side of life. Brought up behind the encircling walls of a series of palaces and spacious pleasure-grounds purposely placed at his disposal, he was given as little opportunity as possible of encountering life in its more sordid aspects. All the more shocking under such circumstances, more especially in the case of a highly sensitive nature such as his, must have been the first revelation of the existence of human misery and suffering.

The sight which, we are given to understand, first accidentally met his gaze was one which is common enough in India—merely that of an ancient beggar moving painfully with bent back and asking with shaky voice for alms. The contrast between his own case, that of a man abundantly endowed with the good things of this world and rejoicing in the full vigour of youth and health, and that of the pitiful beggar, struck deep into his imagination. The other great evils to which man is subject, disease and death—so at least runs the story—were revealed to him on separate occasions in the shape of a sufferer burned with the consuming fire of fever, and of a corpse borne along on a bier and followed by a procession of mourners weeping and beating their breasts.

It matters little, however, whether his perception of the ills to which humanity is heir was actually awakened in the way recorded. It is certain enough that, despite every effort to keep him in ignorance of the more sombre side of life as experienced by the humbler folk in whose midst he dwelt, disillusionment must sooner or later have come.

The story concludes with a fourth incident. Driving out one day he met a wandering ascetic, and, struck with the unusual appearance of his garments and his calm and dignified demeanour, he inquired what manner of man he was. On learning that he was a member of a religious order who had abandoned the life of the world, he was seized with an overmastering desire to follow his example, to leave his life of luxury and ease in order to search out for himself the causes of the unaccountable inequalities in the lot of man, which had been so rudely thrust upon his notice. In the description of the period of his life which follows we see the picture of a man tortured with uncertainty, searching strenuously for an answer to the questions which crowded upon his mind, and we are gradually led up to the final dramatic moment when the veil of ignorance which obscured his spiritual vision was torn asunder and truth stood revealed.

It was only natural that in setting forth upon his quest he should choose the path of asceticism. The ideal of India then as now was renunciation. Of the Brahman it was definitely required that he should spend the latter part of his life in retirement from the world. Indeed, the importance which came to be attached to a rigorous ordering of life is clear from the detailed instructions subsequently drawn up and embodied in the code of Manu, wherein it is laid down that the four stages (Ashramas) into which the life of a Brahman should be divided are those of (1) the Bramacharin or student; (2) the Grihastha or householder; (3) the Vanaprastha or hermit, and (4) the Sannyhasin or wandering ascetic. Asceticism was, indeed, already widely practised and highly developed, no less than thirty-five methods of self-mortification in respect of food and clothing alone being definitely recognised.[1]

So the Prince Siddartha, leaving father and mother and wife and son, donned the robe of a homeless friar and went forth in search of the hidden way, by which man might escape from the ever-revolving cycle of birth, disease, old age, and death. Students of comparative religion will note with interest the parallel which the story of his temptation on the day of his going forth provides, with the temptation of Jesus Christ when He went forth into the wilderness. As he passed

[1] Howells, *The Soul of India*, p. 423.

through the gateway of the palace grounds—so runs the legend—Mara the evil one appeared to him and tempted him, offering him the sovereignty of the world if he would desist from his intention. In the one case as in the other the tempter was rebuked and thrust aside—"Mara! I seek not the sovereignty of the world. I would become a Buddha to make tens of thousands of worlds rejoice." Thereupon Mara left him.

The chief interest of the story of the next six years lies in the fact that self-mortification carried to extremes, which excited interest even in those days of asceticism, was tried and was found wanting. If the detailed accounts of the fastings and penances to which Gautama subjected himself are to be relied upon, there is no doubt that at the end of six years his body was reduced to a withered skeleton scarcely capable of sustaining life. And finding that he was no nearer his goal than when he started, he resolved to give up the fastings and penances which had proved sterile and try other means. So he took his staff and begging-bowl once more, and wandered from place to place, regaining by degrees his strength of body and mind.

At Buddh Gaya, seven miles south of the town of Gaya in the province of Bihar, there stands an ancient temple. At the back of the temple itself may be seen growing from a raised platform an ancient specimen of a pipal tree. A similar tree reputed to be an offshoot of that at Buddh Gaya exists at Anuradhapura, the most famous of the buried cities of Ceylon. I have seen them both and am disposed to agree with the generally accepted view that the latter is the older of the two. There are, indeed, good grounds for believing that the sacred pipal at Anuradhapura, which is generally admitted to be the oldest historical tree in the world, is the actual tree presented by the missionary Emperor Asoka to King Tissa of Ceylon, on the occasion of the introduction of Buddhism to his kingdom two and a half centuries B.C. And if there is less reason for believing that the specimen now preserved at Buddh Gaya is the original tree from which the shoot was cut, it is at least possible that it grew from its roots and that to this extent continuity has been preserved. Be that as it may, for the devout pilgrims who repair yearly to Buddh Gaya from Ceylon, Burma, and Tibet, the sacred Bo-tree is the actual tree beneath which Gautama sat and found salvation. Where mortification of the flesh had failed, profound and prolonged introspection succeeded.

It is recorded how towards evening, after resting during the heat of an April day, Gautama made his way to the foot of the Bodhi-tree. The coming event which was to influence so profoundly the history of the world was heralded by signs and wonders. Mara the evil one appeared arrayed for battle, and with his demon hosts fought fiercely to overcome him who was about to become the Buddha. Threats, temptations, and actual onslaught were alike vain. "The victory was achieved while the sun was yet above the horizon. The Bodhisatva sank into ever deeper and deeper thought. In the first watch of the night he reached the knowledge of Former

States of Being, in the middle watch he obtained the heavenly eye of Omniscient Vision, and in the third watch he grasped the perfect understanding of the Chain of Causation which is the Origin of Evil, and thus at break of day he attained to Perfect Enlightenment."[1]

Here again it matters little whether the circumstances in which the intuitional knowledge came to him were precisely as narrated. Interest centres not so much in the external surroundings amid which perception took place, as in the thing which was perceived. And the thing perceived was enunciated in the famous first sermon known since as the "setting in motion of the wheel of the law," which was delivered some weeks later in the deer park near Benares, now known by the name of Sarnath. In the course of this his first discourse, the Tathāgatha or Blessed One, propounded the four noble truths within which is comprised the essence of his gospel to mankind. This gospel I shall endeavour to explain, but before doing so I will bring this brief narrative of Gautama's life to its close.

The ministry which followed upon the enlightenment described above, lasted for a period of forty-five years, during which the doctrine was elaborated and the order of mendicants founded. The usual practice was for Gautama, accompanied by some of his disciples, of whom Ananda became his most constant companion, to travel over the country during the dry season taking part in discussions, delivering discourses,

[1] A. K. Coomaraswamy, D.Sc., *Buddha and the Gospel of Buddhism*, p. 35.

and making converts. During the rainy season Gautama and his disciples went into retreat either in some well-known cave, or in a *vihara* built in some sheltered grove on the outskirts of some town or village, such, for example, as the famous Veluvana grove, the site of which on the outskirts of the ancient city of Rajagriha may be seen to this day.

Accounts of the forty-five years of his mission upon earth are exceedingly fragmentary, the last few months only of his life being described in any detail, in the *Book of the Great Decease.* The narrative opens with a conversation between an envoy sent by Ajatasatru, king of Magadha, to Gautama, who was at that time residing in a cave on the side of the Vulture's Peak, the most famous of the hills surrounding the city of Rajagriha. The king was contemplating an attack upon his neighbours the Vajjians and was anxious to know what Gautama thought of the project—"for the Buddhas speak nothing untrue"—a sidelight upon the position as a sage to which Gautama had attained. After giving the names of a number of places to which visits were paid, the writer takes us to Beluva in the vicinity of Vesali where the last rainy season was spent. While here Gautama was attacked by a dire sickness and "sharp pains came upon him even unto death." By an effort of the will he threw off the illness, but he realised that his life was drawing to a close.

"I, too, O Ananda, am now grown old, and full of years, my journey is drawing to its close. I have reached my sum of days, I am turning eighty years of age."

Plate 6.

A DIGNITARY OF THE CHURCH, THE UM-DSÉ OF PEMIONGCHI.

At the close of the rainy season he visited a number of villages in the neighbourhood of Vesali, repeating over and over again to the assembled brethren a comprehensive religious discourse. " Such and such is upright conduct; such and such is earnest contemplation; such and such is intelligence. Great becomes the fruit, great the advantage of earnest contemplation when it is set round with upright conduct. Great becomes the fruit, great the advantage of intellect when it is set round with earnest contemplation. The mind set round with intelligence is set quite free from the intoxication of sensuality, from the intoxication of becoming, from the intoxication of delusion, from the intoxication of ignorance."

While at the Chepala shrine at Vesali he prophesied his death in three months' time, and on leaving Vesali he gazed back upon the place and declared, " This will be the last time, Ananda, that the Tathāgatha will behold Vesali." After visiting many places in the neighbourhood of Vesali he proceeded to Pava, where he stayed in the mango grove of Chunda, a worker in metals. After taking a meal prepared by his host he again fell sick, but bearing himself with fortitude took the road to Kusinara. Becoming weary on the way he rested and definitely foretold his death. " And now this day, Ananda, at the third watch of the night, in the Upavattana of Kusinara, in the Sal grove of the Mallians, between the twin Sal trees, the utter passing away of the Tathāgatha will take place."

After bathing in the river Kakuttha he proceeded with a great company of the brethren and reached the Sal grove of Kusinara. Here in conversation with the brethren he decreed that four places should be regarded as places of pilgrimage —the place of his birth, the place where he obtained enlightenment, the place where he first preached the law, and the place of his death. He then gave directions as to the disposal of his body: "as men treat the body of a king of kings, so, Ananda, should they treat the remains of a Tathāgatha." The events of his last hours are recorded in some detail. He despatched Ananda to the Mallas to inform them that his approaching death would take place in the last watch of the night, and bade them come to him in the Sal grove lest they afterwards reproached themselves for failing to visit him on his deathbed. He spent the first watch granting them audience and subsequently converted Subhadda, an old religious mendicant who had long sought after truth. Next he adjured the brethren present if they entertained any doubts with regard to the Buddha, the doctrine, the path, or the method, to speak out boldly in order that he might satisfy them. No one responded, and he then spoke his last words: "Behold now, brethren. I exhort you saying,—'decay is inherent in all component things.' Work out your salvation with diligence!" His death was accompanied by "a mighty earthquake terrible and awe-inspiring: and the thunders of heaven burst forth."

The concluding pages of the *Book of the Great Decease* are occupied with the funeral rites and the subsequent distribution of the relics. On receipt of the news of the death of the Buddha the

Mallas of Kusinara gave orders "to gather together perfumes and garlands and all the music in *Kusinara,*" and for six days they did homage to the remains of the Tathāgatha. On the seventh day his body was carried to the shrine of the Mallas called Makuta-bandhana, and here in due course it was burned upon an elaborate funeral pyre. Claims to a portion of the remains were put in by Ajatasatru, king of Magadha, and seven others. At first the Mallas of Kusinara were unwilling to give up any portion of them, but were finally persuaded to do so by one Dona, a Brahman. And the remains were distributed among the eight applicants, and cairns were set up by each over the sacred relics. And Dona the Brahman retained the vessel in which the remains had been collected and set up a cairn over it. And the Moriyas of Pipphalivana erected a cairn over the embers. Thus there were ten cairns in all.

CHAPTER VII [1]

THE DOCTRINE OF THE THERA VADA

THE process of giving systematised form to the life and teaching of the Buddha was a slow one. The doctrine and the sayings of the Master were handed down orally by many disciples, with the inevitable result that confusion and dissension arose. Mention is made in the Buddhist tradition of three councils, at the first of which, held in the year of Gautama's death, the rules of the order and the doctrine are said to have been expounded by Upali and Ananda respectively, those assembled repeating what was said after them. Thereafter a difference of opinion arose, resulting in the second council a hundred years later and a schism in the church.

The third council is said to have been convened in the reign of Asoka in the year 247 B.C., and the account of it given in the *Mahavamsa* throws a flood of light upon the extent of the confusion which then prevailed. From it we learn that Asoka called up in turn representatives of the different sects, who expounded to him one after another heretical doctrines to the number of

[1] Persons who are repelled by metaphysical discussion are advised to omit this chapter.

more than sixty. Whereupon the king caused them to be expelled from the order; and the number of those who were expelled was sixty thousand. Thereafter we learn how the chief monk in the assembly, the Thera Tissa, the son of Moggali, together with a thousand learned *bhikkus*, made a compilation of the true doctrine, and how he himself " set forth the *Kathavatthuppakarana* refuting the other doctrines." This latter work is to be found in the *Abhidamma*, and a considerable advance was undoubtedly made in the direction of drawing up a recognised canon of the Scriptures. But it is doubtful, as has already been pointed out, how far, if at all, these compilations were committed to writing even now; and despite the drastic action of Asoka, sects continued to make their appearance and to flourish.

Apart from the numerous sects, Buddhism is divided into two main schools, and it is with these only that we need concern ourselves. They are known respectively as the Hinayāna or " little vehicle," and the Mahayāna or " great vehicle." And in accordance with his temperament it is to the one or the other of these craft that the Buddhist looks to carry him across the ocean of life to the great peace which lies beyond. The former is so called mainly because, according to its tenets, man can only obtain salvation by the help of his own unaided intellectual powers. There is no scope within its doctrine for a Saviour whom man may worship and to whom he may offer prayer. He must rely exclusively upon himself. Its sacred canon is in Pali, and it is claimed for it that it represents the original teaching of Gautama himself—in other words, that it is the orthodox exposition of Buddhism. I shall refer to it as the Thera Vada—" the way of the Elders " —because this is the title which its adherents themselves prefer, the term Hinayāna being objectionable to them.

The Mahayāna school, which was of somewhat later date, developed a theology, its adherents demanding a Saviour to whom they might turn to assist them across the waters of life's troubled sea to the far distant shore which—so thought the adherents of this school—man by his own unaided effort could scarcely hope to reach. Under such circumstances the pure intellectualism, by the aid of which alone in the case of the Thera Vada the voyage was to be accomplished, was obviously insufficient, and faith, worship, and devotion were the oars with which the adherents of the Mahayāna sought to drive their craft across the sea. I shall refer to the rise and teaching of this school later; for the present I propose to confine myself to the doctrine of the Thera Vada.

The four noble truths are the four pillars of the Thera Vada. The first of these was a mere asseveration that all existence was suffering and therefore evil—" *Idan pi dukkha,*" " here verily is ill." In the second noble truth the source of suffering was disclosed—" Verily it is the craving thirst that causes the renewal of becomings, that is accompanied by sensual delights and seeks satisfaction now here now there—that is to say, the craving for the gratification of the senses or the craving for prosperity." In a word, *desire.* The third noble truth proclaimed that suffering could be brought to an end by the drying up of its source, that is to say, by the complete destruction of desire. The whole value of the gospel lies enshrined in the fourth truth, since it is in this last truth that the means by which the destruction of desire can be achieved, are revealed. "As they stand by themselves with nothing further added the first three truths are as barren as is any other piece of purely intellectual knowledge that has not yet been brought into practical, actual relation with the life of man; but when to their statement of what requires to be done there are appended full directions as to how the necessary work may surely and certainly be accomplished, we have given to us all the materials we have any right to ask from a philosophy from ethics or from a religion."[1] And what is the path that leads to the destruction of desire and so to the cessation of suffering? "Verily it is this Noble Eightfold Path, that is to say, Right Seeing, Right Aspiring, Right Doing, Right Speaking, Right Living, Right Endeavouring, Right Remembering, and Right Reflecting."

It will be seen that this solution of the problem is an ethical one. The Path is a middle way. If undue attachment to the pleasures of the world is condemned as harmful, habitual devotion to self-mortification is equally rejected as unprofitable. The one way to destroy desire and so escape from the evil of existence, entanglement in the ever-revolving cycle of birth, old age and

[1] *The Four Noble Truths,* by the Bhikkhu Silacara.

death, is the right ordering of conduct in thought, in word, and in deed. The monasticism which is a feature of Buddhism was a natural corollary of this view, since a monastic life, while avoiding the rigours of asceticism, provided facilities for undisturbed meditation and shielded those who adopted it against undue contact with the pleasures and allurements of the world. I shall have more to say on the value of the ethics of Buddhism later on. But the ethics were closely associated with an explanation not of the origin of human existence—that was beyond explanation—but of its nature; an explanation which is one of the cardinal pillars of the doctrine and to which, therefore, I shall have to devote some space.

If men had been content to bow in blind obedience to authority and to tread in unquestioning faith the path laid down, the four noble truths would have constituted the last word on Buddhism. But man is by nature undisciplined and has seldom been content passively to obey. Least of all was it to be expected that the race which was capable of evolving the famous six systems should rest content with the mere statement that existence was evil, that it was due to certain causes, that these causes could be made to cease and existence consequently be brought to an end, by the adoption of certain arbitrary standards of conduct dubbed RIGHT. It was, indeed, inevitable that Buddhism should become a system. How far the system was evolved by Buddha himself in his discourses and his discussion with his disciples and how far it was elaborated after his death is a matter for speculation. For most men it is immaterial. What is material is the nature of the system.

What, then, of the metaphysics of Buddhism? A man would not have to be curious above the average if, on learning that he could bring to an end his earthly existence, he wished to know what his state would then be. The answer given by Buddhism to such a question is that he would have attained Nirvana. But this answer, far from satisfying his curiosity, is calculated merely to arouse it further, since it is precisely over the meaning of this term that controversy has raged most fiercely.

Assuming the premises from which Buddhism starts, I find it difficult to escape from the conclusion that Nirvana is equivalent to annihilation. To begin with, Buddhism denies the existence of the soul or of anything corresponding to it. It denies static existence altogether. Strictly speaking, there is, according to the teaching of the Thera Vada, no such state or condition as that suggested by the word existence. Everything is a "becoming." The sum total of phenomena is an endless and beginningless chain of cause and effect. The thing commonly spoken of as an individual *being* is not a being at all—it is a *succession* of infinitesimal instants of consciousness. This is known as the doctrine of impermanence.

Something there must be which keeps the wheel of becoming in motion, and this something must be of supreme importance in the Buddhist system, since its removal (if possible) would bring the eternal becoming to rest—and Nirvana would ensue. What, then, is this supremely important principle which keeps the wheel of life in motion? To that question Gautama replies —"the law of universal causation." This is a far more momentous pronouncement than at first sight appears. Immediately and once and for all it expunged God viewed as a First Cause, and the Soul—individual or universal—from the slate of possibility. "The pilgrimage of beings (*saṁsara*), my disciples, has its beginning in eternity. No opening (First Cause) can be discovered whence proceeding creatures fettered by a thirst for being stray and wander."

The idea itself was not new; it was the basis of the widely accepted doctrine of karma which asserted that every action (in the widest possible sense of the word, *i.e.* by thought, word, or deed) was automatically followed sooner or later, in this life or in a subsequent existence, by reward or retribution; in other words, the sequence of cause and effect was inexorable. But it was Buddhism which, driving the doctrine of causality to its logical conclusion, exalted it above all gods and found in it the supreme and sole explanation of all phenomena. It was in the third watch of the night of his enlightenment that Gautama is said to have seen as in a flash the chain of causation which gives rise to suffering. It was, indeed, in respect of the existence of suffering in particular that knowledge of the law of universal causation was first gained, as set forth in a sutra of the Sanskrit Canon:

"In the third night of his meditation the

would-be Buddha examined the natures of all living beings and asked himself, 'What is the cause of old age and death ?' He then replied to himself saying: 'I know that old age and death are brought about by birth which is not produced by a god or by itself or by chance, but is the effect of causes and conditions, that is to say, it is the outcome of *karma* in the realm of Desire, of Form, and of Formlessness. Again, whence arise the *karmas* of these three realms ? They arise from the fourfold attachments. Whence arise those attachments ? Forsooth from desire. Whence arises desire ?. From sensation. And whence arises sensation ? From contact. Whence arises contact ? From the six organs of sense. Whence arise the six organs of sense ? From name and form. Whence arise name and form ? From consciousness. Whence arises consciousness ? From the *samskaras* or conformations. Whence arise conformations ? From ignorance.' " This is the famous Chain of Causation known as the twelve *nidanas*. The significance may be more easily grasped if it is thrown into tabular form as follows :

THE TWELVE NIDANAS

A. Cause and Effect in the Past and the Present :

1. Avidya (ignorance)	Past cause.
2. Samskara (mental activity)	
3. Vijnana (consciousness)	Present effect.
4. Namarupa (name and form)	
5. Shadayatana (sixfold organ)	
6. Sparsa (contact)	
7. Vedana (sensation)	

B. Cause and Effect in the Present and the Future :

8. Trishna (desire) 9. Upadana (clinging) 10. Bhava (existence)	Present cause.
11. Jati (birth) 12. Jaramaranam (old age and death)	Future effect.

For a complete explanation of the exact relationship between these links of the Chain of Causation, it would be necessary to embark upon a detailed discussion of the full significance of each of the terms employed, without which the English equivalents given above are not altogether illuminating, and may, indeed, in some cases prove to be actually misleading. But to do so would be to overweight these pages. Neither are the details of the chain, such as the precise number of its links or the order in which they occur, of fundamental importance. In the Buddhist canon itself both the number and the order of the Nidanas vary. For example, in the *Maha-Nidana Suttanta* or " the great discourse on Causation " in the *Digha Nikaya*, the first two in the above table are omitted, and it is stated that Name and Form are the cause of consciousness and *vice versa*. Ignorance is usually taken as a starting-point " merely for the purpose of exposition and not because it is itself causeless and not determined at any stage by the similarly repeating events of preceding stages." [1] What is of fundamental importance is a recognition of the

[1] S. N. Das Gupta. For the table given above I am indebted to Mr. Yamakami Sögen's *Systems of Buddhistic Thought*, published by the University of Calcutta.

Plate 7.

A VENERABLE PRELATE, THE DORJÉ-LOPEN OF FADUNG.

principle that nothing occurs without a cause, and that so long as such and such a cause exists such and such a result must follow—and that this has always been so and always will be so, without possibility of it being otherwise. The essential importance of a recognition of the principle as opposed to any particular application of it, is made clear by a passage in the *Mahapadana Suttanta*, the significance of which is enhanced by the fact that it follows immediately after a detailed rehearsal of the twelve *nidanas* : " Coming to be, coming to be ! At that thought, brethren, there arose to Vipassi the Bodhisat a vision into things not before called to mind, and knowledge arose, reason arose, wisdom arose, light arose." [1]

In the twelve *nidanas*, then, we see the application of the principle of causality to the particular problem of evil, and its significance may be appreciated at a glance by a reference to the table which has been given above. If it be admitted that such things as consciousness are the present effects of past causes, and that these present effects are inseparable from other things such as craving, which in their turn are the causes of future effects such as birth, it will be seen that as surely as the future dissolves eternally into the present, and the present fades eternally into the past, so certainly must the operation of these causes and effects eternally continue.

The human mind conditioned by time and

[1] In this case the discourse on causation is put into the mouth of Vipassi, the first of six forerunners of Gautama. Like everything else in Buddhism, Buddhas recur. They all teach precisely the same doctrine ; and their recurrence is necessary for the salvation of a forgetful world.

space plays with eternity as an abstract idea; but if it tries to seize hold of the idea and subject it to analysis, it is driven to substitute for the real thing that which appears to possess similar characteristics in its own conditioned world of experience. And since the essence of eternity is beginninglessness and endlessness, the human mind takes as its counterpart that which in the world of time and space appears to be without beginning and without end, namely, the circle. It was thus, no doubt, that the doctrine of causality as exemplified by the twelve *nidanas*, came to be known as the "Wheel of Causation." Bowing to the same necessity we may seek to illustrate the operation of the principle by analogy, and to represent the metaphysical conception in terms of physics by likening it to a wheel of twelve spokes, each of which is in perpetual motion, the motion of each being dependent on the motion of the one next to it. If, then, a single spoke can be knocked out, the mechanism will be destroyed and the whole will come to rest. In other words, we have an endless chain (wheel) which must continue in perpetual motion (revolving) unless one link (spoke) at least can be broken.

That there are links in the chain which can be broken is precisely what is asserted in the third Noble Truth. How they can be broken is taught in the fourth Noble Truth wherein is set forth the Noble Eightfold Path. A consideration of the constituent stages of the eightfold path suggests that salvation may be obtained by reason or by faith—by faith in the Buddha, the Doctrine, and the Order, which will enable a man to destroy the link in the chain called *trishna* (desire): by reason, which will enable a man to destroy the link called *avidya* (ignorance). Ignorance of what? it may be asked. Of the impermanence of all things, of the fact that there is no such thing in the world of experience as a state of being—that everything is a state of becoming. For it is the non-realisation of this truth that gives rise to the idea of "I" and "mine," which idea in its turn gives rise to craving and grasping, whence springs the will to live which is the sole support of life. And from life, to make use of the Buddhist formula, arise "old age and death, sorrow, lamentations, pain, grief, despair. Such is the coming to be of this entire body of Ill."

Thus, then, may a man break an essential link in the chain and so bring the whole wheel of causation and the state of becoming to rest so far as he is concerned. And since he himself is only a succession of infinitesimal instants of consciousness, and that succession has now been brought to an end, what is there left? Can logic provide any other answer to the question than that there is nothing left? Look at it from a slightly different point of view. Man is merely a coming together of certain properties or qualities categorised by Buddhists under five heads termed *skandhas*—(1) *rupa*, organised body, (2) *vedana*, sensation, (3) *samjna*, perception, (4) *samskara*, discrimination, and (5) *vignana*, consciousness. When physical dissolution takes place these components disperse leaving no residue. And since there is no residue there can be no soul. This is illustrated by Nagasena the sage in reply to a question of King Milinda, by the famous simile of the chariot and its parts. The king had scoffed at the statement of the sage that the name Nagasena, like any other name, was merely a convenient designation in common use, and that its use did not predicate any permanent individuality. The sage listened patiently to the declamation of the royal controversialist, and at length asked if he could explain the nature of the chariot in which he had driven to see him? "Is it the pole that is the chariot?" The king said that it was not. "Is it then the axle that is the chariot?" Again the king denied it. "Is it the wheels or the framework, or the ropes, or the yoke, or the spokes of the wheels, or the goad that are the chariot?" persisted the sage. The king confessed that it was none of these. "Is it then all these parts of it that are the chariot?" Again the king replied that it was not. "But is there anything outside them that is the chariot?" Milinda admitted that there was not; and Nagasena declared that he was unable then to discover any chariot—that the word was a mere empty sound. At which the king dissented, saying that it was on account of its having all these things, the pole, the axle, the wheels, and so on, that it came under the generally understood term, the designation in common use of "chariot." The sage applauded him, saying that he had rightly grasped the meaning of "chariot"; and added that in the same way it was on account of the various kinds of organic matter in a human body and the five constituent elements of being that he himself came under the generally understood term, the designation in common use of "Nagasena."[1]

It would, therefore, appear at first sight that the fear of re-birth which it is the main object of Buddhism to escape, can be nothing but a figment of the imagination. If there is nothing left over when the components of man disperse, there is nothing to be re-born. But this is not so; and in order to make clear the Buddhist theory of re-birth reference must be made to the meaning of *karma.* When a man dies there will be left over from his life's activities, so to speak, a certain balance of unrequited action. It may be good action or it may be bad action; but in accordance with the doctrine of *karma* reward or retribution must follow automatically. And it is that fundamental necessity which causes a fresh assemblage of *skandhas* for the working out of the unexhausted *karma.* Re-birth, then, is a mere manifestation of the effects of certain causes. The link between death and re-birth is impersonal and imponderable. None of the words ordinarily used in this connection is strictly applicable. There can be no metempsychosis where there is no soul. There can be no re-incarnation where there is no "being" to take on flesh. There can be no transmigration where there is no entity to migrate. "Suppose a man were to light a lamp from another lamp, can it be said," asked Nagasena, "that the one transmigrates from, or to, the other?" To which Milinda the king replied, "Certainly not." "Just so, great king, is re-birth without transmigration."

[1] *The Questions of King Milinda,* Book II. chap. i.

Nevertheless wherever there is a " becoming " (conscious life) there is suffering, as stated in the First Noble Truth ; and it matters little to the man who is the victim at any one given moment, what the previous history-sheet of the suffering has been. It is desirable as a general proposition that suffering should cease ; and it is to this end that Buddha preached. Suppose, then, that by treading the Noble Eightfold Path a man so lives that his *karma* works itself out, leaving over no balance of unrequited action at the moment of death ; then he leaves behind him nothing capable of causing a reassemblage of the five *skandhas*. And he has *pro tanto* reduced the sum total of existence.

Suppose further that in a given generation every sentient being was equally successful in achievement. Then there would be no further assemblage of the components of existence at all. The revolving wheel of life would have ceased and all mankind would have attained to Nirvana. There would be no " being " nor any " becoming." Indeed it is difficult to see what there would be. And so we are inexorably driven to the same conclusion as before, namely, that Nirvana is another word for annihilation.

But it is precisely against any such conclusion that the mind of man most determinedly revolts. The will to persist is strong in him ; and the theologians willing enough to concede something to a weakness of humanity so universally prevalent, temporised on the question. Buddha himself, while refusing to discuss the question of life apart from the world of becoming, equally refused to close the door upon the possibilities of a future beyond the world of experience. "I have not revealed that the Arahat (he who has attained Nirvana) exists after death, I have not revealed that he does not exist; I have not revealed that he at once exists and does not exist after death, nor that he neither exists nor does not exist after death." And he added that he had not done so because speculation on the subject did not tend to the absence of passion or to supreme wisdom. The state of a man set free from the cycle of existence could be discussed with no more advantage than the state of a flame that has been blown out, for when all conditions are cut off all matter for discussion is cut off also.[1]

And seizing upon the concession thus made to human hopes, other authorities did not hesitate to depict Nirvana as a condition of perfect bliss. Take for example the exposition of a Buddhist *bhikkhu* of the present day. Buddha's silence with regard to a future state he attributes not to ignorance, but to the profoundest knowledge—"the knowledge that nothing can be said of that Beyond-the-World in the speech of this Within-the-World that will not in some way be false, misleading, untrue." He then goes on to assert that those who have attained to the supreme Wisdom *know* that while this land in which men live is impermanent, a world of *becoming*, the land of Nirvana is permanent, a world of *being*, "constant, unchanging, ever the same." While this world is subject to suffering, "that land of Nirvana is altogether free from any sorrow or pain."

[1] The quotation from the *Majjhima Nikaya* is taken from Dr. Ananda Coomaraswamy's *Buddha and the Gospel of Buddhism*, p. 120.

And he concludes with the most definite assurances—"No, Nirvana is not nothing: it only so far surpasses any good of earth that one can give it no fitting name—no name that will not make it less than what it really is; it only so much excels all happiness of earth that one can assign it no proper and suitable form. Thus, beyond all names, all forms that we can give, it yet *is*. Truly no tongue may tell *what* it is; but this is so, not because it is nothing, but because it is something so much greater and grander than anything known to our world that every attempt to phrase that greatness and grandeur in earthly speech perforce must fail and fall short of expressing its supreme, its incomparable reality."

It is more than likely that if any thoughtful Christian was asked to give his idea of Heaven, he would do so in very similar words; and it is a little difficult to reconcile the state of Nirvana as here described with the denial both of a supreme and of an individual soul. But it bears out what I have said as to the unwillingness even of Buddhists themselves, to accept without qualification the pure rationalism upon which Buddhism is primarily based.[1]

[1] The quotation is from a monograph entitled *The Four Noble Truths*, by the Bhikkhu Silacara. The author is, I believe, a Scotsman who has been converted to Buddhism, and it is possible that his conception of Nirvana is coloured by previous ideas about Heaven. But Nirvana is described as a state of perfect bliss in many works by Asiatic Buddhists. The Siamese, for example, always refer to it as something existing, according to Mr. H. Alabaster, who quotes the following from *Buddha's Nirvana*. Nirvana is "a place of comfort where there is no care, lovely is it the glorious realm of Nirvana." See his *The Wheel of the Law*. And Mr. K. J. Saunders gives as a reason for omitting passages dealing with the nature of Nirvana from his anthology of Buddhist verse entitled *The Heart of Buddhism*, the possibility of supporting any of the current theories concerning it from the Sacred Books.

The word Nirvana has, indeed, been the subject of much learned disputation, both from an etymological and from a philosophical point of view; but there is little profit to others than specialists in considering it, for the reason, if for no other, that "for our European logic it is existence outside all sensation, all desire, all will, all function—an existence in fact without life, which our mentality refuses to grasp."[1] And I have referred to the tendency of Buddhism to temporise on the question of annihilation, mainly because it leads up to my final contention, namely, that just as it was inevitable that Buddhism should become a system, so it was inevitable that despite its denial of a supreme and an individual soul, it should become a religion.

The explanation of a paradox so profound must be sought in certain characteristics inherent in mankind. The metaphysics of Thera Vada Buddhism possess a fascinating interest for those who are content to live on a plane of frigid intellectualism. But their number is necessarily limited. Man in the mass lives far more on an emotional than on an intellectual plane. And man's emotional nature demands something to worship. What, then, more natural than that for vast numbers of Buddhists, Gautama Buddha himself should have supplied the central object for the adoration which their emotional nature craved? Nowhere, perhaps, has this metamorphosis been carried further than in Sikhim and Tibet. But it would be a mistake to suppose

[1] Introduction by J. Deniker to *The Gods of Northern Buddhism*, by Alice Getty.

that the process had not made great strides in India itself, before ever the doctrine penetrated the mountain fastnesses which ring in the land of its birth. I shall have something to say upon the circumstances which were responsible for such changes later on. First let me introduce the reader to the Buddhism which is actually practised in Sikhim at the present day.

CHAPTER VIII

THROUGH THE FOREST TO TASHIDING

FROM Darjeeling one may cross into Sikhim at different points. The route *via* Phalut which has already been described is by no means the most direct. One may drop from Darjeeling itself six thousand feet to the Rungeet river, crossed here by a foot-bridge suspended giddily between Bengal and Sikhim; or one may strike the valley of the Rungeet farther west, approaching the frontier by the picturesque little village of Singla Bazar. Or, again, one may make one's way to the Tista valley and ascend along the river's banks to the frontier at Rungpo. The routes which cross the Rungeet river give the most direct access to the lovely forest-clad spurs and ranges upon which the priesthood of the country has plotted out the picturesque monasteries and shrines of Tibetan Buddhism.

They have shown a fine perception of the beautiful in nature, for the forest here possesses a singular attraction. It is essentially a place of moods. At times it is intensely still. Bright sunlight filters through a fretwork of rich green foliage, lighting up splashes of colour where flowers grow softly cushioned on the slopes of moss-covered banks. Butterflies of many hues flash like living jewels from flower to flower, dancing a mad dance of ephemeral existence under the stimulus of the sun-laden air. Every variety of foliage is to be seen, from the delicate feathery leaf of the acacia to the broad polished leaf of the upstanding Sāl. A host of parasitic growths clings to all the larger trees, ferns, orchids, lichens, and moss. Here and there the dark green pothos grips the trunks of the tallest trees in sinister embrace. Now and then a curious phenomenon may be observed. On the stillest day a single leaf or frond will suddenly start moving in wild gyrations while all else remains unmoved. "Shaitan," say the superstitious mountain folk; "An atmospheric eddy," grunts the native forester, contemptuous of supernatural explanations in his superior knowledge of scientific forest lore.

Such is the forest in smiling mood. Suddenly there comes a change. The sunlight vanishes and light is swallowed up in shade. The smile is gone and nature seems to frown. A chill draught passes through the trees. Wreaths of mist rush by, winding about the moss-grown trunks like grave-clothes about a corpse. Colour has fled and has left only a picture in sombre half-tones. With the same suddenness with which it arose the wind dies down, leaving a solemn hush brooding heavily over the world. One feels irresistibly that this immense silence must be broken only by sound in a minor key. One imagines the mournful strains of Sibelius's *Valse triste* or of Grieg's *Mort d'Ase* sighing their way across the scene and evoking echoes of infinite sadness from the soul of this dim world of shadows. With an appropriateness that is startling, a deep long-drawn drone comes rolling through the air—a curious sound which is certainly not musical in the ordinarily accepted meaning of that word, but which is equally certainly harmonious in that it blends so perfectly with the *mise-en-scène*. When listening to it I have realised its relationship to nature. It is the sound which would be produced by the hum of myriads of bees swarming through the forest. It is actually produced by the Tibetan *ra-dong*, an immense horn, usually from six to eight feet in length, two or more of which are part of the property of every monastery. It is the lama's welcome to the honoured guest.

From the heights above the elbow of the Rungeet river one can see at a single glance half-a-dozen or more of the most famous monasteries of Sikhim—Pemiongchi, "the sublime perfect lotus," Sanga Chelling, "the place of secret spells," Dubdi, "the hermit's cell," Tashiding, "the elevated central glory," Dalling, "the stony site," and Senan, "the suppressor of intense fear," among them.

Let me hasten to explain, lest this string of names catches the eye of a petulant philologist, that I have adopted the spelling given in the Gazetteer of Sikhim, which is presumably upon a phonetic basis, since the actual transliteration of the vernacular name in the case of Sanga Chelling is given as "gsang-sngags-chlosgling." However superior this latter form may be from a strictly scientific point of view, it suffers from the patent disadvantage that it is calculated to raise doubts in the mind of the uninformed, as to the precise sounds which they should give vent to, should they desire to make mention of the place out loud. This seems to me to provide ample justification for sacrificing pedantry to convenience. But I digress. Of the monasteries mentioned Dubdi is the oldest, and Tashiding and Pemiongchi are the most famous. The latter is also the richest and largest, the number of monks attached to it being over a hundred.

Tashiding has the merit (from the lama's point of view) of being particularly difficult of access. The word denoting a monastery is *gompa*, the meaning of which is "a solitary place"; and the true gompa consists of a colony of lamas living round a collection of temple buildings apart from the world. Tashiding conforms to these specifications. It stands in splendid isolation upon the summit of a precipitous and densely-wooded spur at the apex of an acute angle formed by the junction of the Rungeet and Rathong rivers. From the little bungalow of Kuzing, where we spent the night before embarking upon a visit, it could be seen crowning a rugged cone which rose abruptly from the valley bottom, as from the depths of a vast pit. In a straight line the distance appeared a negligible quantity; but the only means of crossing the intervening space was by descending to the Rungeet river, and then scaling the almost perpendicular heights on the farther side.

The track which we followed was steep and stony, and we slid and stumbled down an uneven

Plate 8.

A SIKHIM HOMESTEAD.

plane inclined at something a good deal more than forty-five degrees. But it was not until we had progressed some distance, that we realised fully the meaning of the warning which we had received, that Tashiding was "off the track." This we did when we overtook a party of villagers from Kuzing, slashing and hacking a pathway for us with their business-like kukries, through the dense thickets of aromatic vegetation that covered the mountain side. All possibility of misunderstanding was finally disposed of when we reached the river and saw the slender bamboo bridge, which had been constructed during the night that we might pass dry-shod over it.

As we gradually neared the top on the far side the silence of the groves was broken, first by the long-drawn note of the ra-dong, and then by an arresting confusion of sounds out of which the blare of horns, the clash of cymbals, and the boom of drums emerged triumphant. The picture which gradually outlined itself through the trees presented a feast of colour. Lamas robed in flowing garments of subdued crimson, stood grouped artistically about a roughly-built gateway of weather-worn stone, giving access to a large enclosure. The blue-grey smoke of burning wormwood rose from stone-mounted braziers, and in the background a collection of chortens stood out in pleasing geometric outline against the sky. At our approach the lamas formed up in procession headed by the band, and to the accompaniment of music we entered the monastery enclosure. Leaving the chortens on our right hand in accordance with ritualistic requirement, we proceeded to the main temple building.

The temple of Sikhim is a two-storied oblong building with a roof of thatch, or sometimes in these prosaic days, alas! of corrugated iron. The lower story consists of a hall and vestibule known as the Lha-khang or house of prayer, and varies little in arrangement and design. The vestibule which gives access to the main hall contains large images of grotesque appearance, and sometimes one or more immense prayer cylinders. From the vestibule a massive wooden door gives entrance to the main hall, which is divided into three parts by two rows of pillars forming a central aisle, which runs from the doorway to the altar at the far end. The size of this hall varies, the largest which I have seen being that at Pemiongchi, which measures roughly eighty feet by forty feet and has four pillars in each row. Most of those which I have visited are somewhat smaller, and have only three pillars on either side of the central aisle. The walls and ceiling are usually covered with frescoes of gods and demons in brilliant colours, sometimes, but not always, of considerable antiquity. On each side of the central aisle run long, low stools, on which the lamas sit cross-legged and facing one another, when taking part in a service. At the end of each of these stools nearest the altar is a raised seat—that on the right as you face the altar, for the spiritual head of the monastery, and that on the left facing him, for the temporal head, who acts as chief chorister and leads the service. At the end of the right-hand stool nearest the door, is another slightly raised seat for a lama who officiates as a marshal, and whose duty it is to see that discipline is maintained.

Three large gilded idols look down with unseeing eyes from niches above the altar. These are usually Gautama Buddha in the centre and Guru Rimpoché and Cheresi on the left and right respectively, as one faces the altar. Guru Rimpoché, the Tibetan name of the Indian monk Guru Padma Sambhava, is venerated throughout the Eastern Himalayas as the founder of Lamaism. His story is told hereafter. Cheresi, the Tibetan form of Avalokitesvara, is the god of mercy and patron god of Lamaism and of Tibet. He is sometimes represented by an image with four hands, and sometimes by one with eleven heads and innumerable arms, each with an eye in the palm. But he still walks the earth in human form, being incarnate in the Dalai Lama. He is said to have brought forth the prayer, "Om mani padme, hum!" which either actually or symbolically, by means of thousands of prayer cylinders and prayer flags, is repeated millions of times a day throughout Tibet and the adjacent countries.

The upper story, which is reached by a staircase running up the outside of the building, usually contains the library. The two great books which every monastery aspires to, but does not always succeed in possessing, are the *Kahgyur* or "The Translated Commandments," and the *Teng-yur* or "The Translated Doctrinal Commentaries." The former consists of a hundred and eight volumes, the latter of more than two hundred. These volumes are attracting considerable attention at the present time, recent researches by the late Dr. Satis Chandra Vidyabhusana among others, having shown that they contain information of great value with regard to ancient Indian philosophy and tradition. The late Dr. Vidyabhusana was engaged at the time of his death, in drawing up a topical index of them, which would be of the greatest assistance to scholars desiring to explore this prodigious work, "comprising material so vast," in the opinion of the Calcutta University Commission, presided over by Sir Michael Sadler, K.C.S.I., "as to furnish ample occupation to an army of scholars and investigators for a generation."[1] In addition to the book there is often a number of images forming a heterogeneous collection of figures of gods, demi-gods, demons, and canonised lamas.

[1] *Report of the Calcutta University Commission*, 1917–1919, vol. ii. p. 100.

CHAPTER IX

LAMAISM IN PRACTICE

IT was to the Lha-khang that we were first escorted by the lamas of Tashiding. Passing through the vestibule, which contained five enormous prayer cylinders, we entered the main hall, and I was conducted to a seat placed at right angles to the altar and behind the right-hand row of pillars forming the central aisle. It was the seat ordinarily reserved for His Highness the Maharaja of Sikhim. In front of me was placed a small altar, on which stood a vase of flowers and a solitary wick burning in a bowl of ghee. It happened to be Sunday, and the Elder, already a little doubtful, I think, of the propriety of a professing Presbyterian taking part even as an onlooker, in the highly ritualistic service of the Lamaist Church, was not a little scandalised at this, my unexpected apotheosis.

The service held in the Lha-khang is curiously satisfying to the senses. The dim light is restful, and the rows of lamps, consisting of small bowls of ghee in which float burning wicks, shed a subdued light upon the altar and tone down both colour and outline of the gilded images before which they burn. The air is faintly perfumed with the scent of flowers. In the half light—daylight is admitted only through the door—the crimson robes of the seated lamas, blend with the brighter colours of the frescoes on the pillars and the walls. At the opening of the service the attention of the deities is invoked by music—a wild appeal on cymbals, horns, conchs, and drums, swelling in volume and increasing in tumultuousness as it works up gradually towards a crashing climax. Then follows a prayer intoned in soft deep cadence by the lamas chanting in unison. This method of invocation practised in the monasteries throughout Tibet, is characterised by a tone and rhythm which stamp it indelibly upon the memory. Once heard it is never forgotten. When I first attended a service in a Sikhim monastery, all but twenty years had passed since I had been present at a similar service at the famous monastery of Hemis in Ladakh; yet so vividly did the first few notes recall the earlier experience, that the whole intervening tale of years seemed blotted out, and it was as though time had ceased to be. As the prayer rolls forth, the deep-throated voices of the worshippers rise and fall like the surge of a rolling sea. The prayers are punctuated by bursts of sound, the roll of drum and the crash of cymbal, and then again there rises on the air the blare of horns and the wild drone of the ra-dong.

After the sonorous chanting of the prayers the chief lama rose, and taking a white scarf, held it up before the great golden image of the Buddha and asked his blessing. He then brought it and placed it upon my shoulders. With a penetrating crash of music the service came to an end.

It is a strange religion this Lamaism of Tibet. One sees in it the soul of man groping painfully after truth, through a morass of formalism and superstition. For a few there runs through it a core of metaphysic. In the *adhi* Buddha, acknowledged by some of the schools of Lamaism, one perceives the conception of a First Cause—a conception akin to that of Brahman (the Absolute) of the Hindus. But for the vast majority of the people Lamaism is a confused medley of demonology, magic, and superstition. There is a whole world of spirits, some of whom have to be propitiated and others supplicated. There is an immense and imposing hierarchy of lamas who, having influence in these vast extra-terrestrial regions, have to be paid for services rendered. Above all, there is merit to be acquired and accumulated by the construction of a chorten, the addition of a stone to the cairns and mendongs[1] which dot the country, or more easily by the interminable repetition of the invocation, "Om mani padme, hum!"—"Hail to the jewel in the Lotus, hail!"

Study the frescoes which adorn the monastery walls and you will find one which, by reason of the frequency with which it appears, soon becomes familiar. Its peculiar interest is due to the intimation which it conveys, that through the bewildering maze of Lamaism there runs the thread of karma and re-birth, which forms the

[1] A thick wall of stones, the outer ones being inscribed with the invocation.

universal warp upon which the various tapestries of Indo-Aryan philosophy are woven. It is a curious circular picture divided into three concentric disks, in the innermost of which are representations of a pig, a cock, and a snake. The outer division runs like a ribbon round the whole and contains a series of figures male and female at regular intervals. The space between the inner and outer—the largest of the three—is divided by radii into six compartments, each containing a medley of figures, animal, human, devilish, and divine. These six compartments, you will be told, represent the six worlds into which a person may be re-born, Heaven being depicted at the top and Hell at the bottom of the picture. On the left as one faces it are shown the animal and human worlds, and on the right the worlds of the tantalised ghosts and of the spirits who are not gods. If during any one existence a man's actions show a credit balance of merit, he is re-born in Heaven, in the world of spirits, or in the human world according to the value of the balance. If, on the other hand, his life's history sheet shows a balance of evil, he is re-born in the animal world, the world of tantalised ghosts, or in Hell.

The pig, the cock, and the snake in the central disk represent the three original sins, ignorance, lust, and anger, by avoiding which virtue is acquired and merit accumulated.

The figures in the outer circle symbolise the twelve *nidanas* or causes of re-birth, ignorance (*avidya*), desire (*trishna*), etc. They encircle the universe in an endless chain, the *result* of one cause being the *cause* of the next, and so on. The whole of this striking work, known as the *si-pa-hi-khor-lo* or "wheel of life," constitutes a pictorial expression of the philosophic conception of an inexorable recurring cycle of existence, which appalled the thinkers of India more than two thousand years ago, and which resulted in the elaboration of the great systems of Indian philosophy, as well as of Buddhism, all devoted to discovering and marking out avenues of escape.

It will be observed, however, that the picture contains no indication of the avenue of escape which Buddha found and preached to men. The circle is endless. The *nidanas* chase one another ceaselessly round the six worlds. The gods in Heaven are subject to the same law of karma as the tortured souls in the nethermost hell. Individuals pass in interminable procession from world to world, helpless in the relentless grip of varying but eternal *life.*

The *summum bonum* which it offers is a period of joyous existence in the world of the gods. The tortures of the damned in the world of the tantalised ghosts—a region in which the unfortunate being grows a huge body, at all times gnawed by hunger and thirst which cannot be satisfied, firstly, because of the microscopic dimensions of its mouth and throat, and, secondly, because such sustenance as is taken in by these organs, is immediately transformed into knives and saws which tear the stomach, and work their way painfully outward through the tortured flesh—and in the still more terrifying hell are depicted with a wealth of realism which is sufficient to drive the people, if not to good deeds, at least to fierce and sustained activity in the mechanical accumulation of merit by means of the prayer cylinder.

But while it is probable that it is upon the achievement of re-birth in the highest of the six worlds—more probably still, perhaps, upon the avoidance of a descent into hell—that the mind of the average villager is set as he twirls his prayer cylinder, or tells his beads, it is also true that the highest aim is vaguely recognised to be escape from existence altogether. And with an extraordinary perversity of intelligence the Noble Eightfold Path laid down by Gautama Buddha, has been transformed into a single narrow track—the infinite reiteration either verbally or mechanically of the mystic incantation " Om mani padme, hum ! "

In its literal meaning this sentence is a salutation to the patron deity of Tibet, Cheresi, who is popularly supposed to have been born from a lotus-flower. But it has also a mystic meaning of profound significance, for the repetition of the syllables of which it is composed bars the doors of the various worlds of existence—*om* of the heavenly world, *ma* of the world of spirits, *ni* of the human world, *pad* of the animal world, *me* of the world of tantalised ghosts, and *hum* of the spaces of hell. Hence the fascination of the prayer cylinder for lama and layman alike. Hence the gigantic prayer barrels, often eight or nine feet in height, which are a feature of every monastery. Hence the diligence and per-

Plate 9.

A MONSTER PRAYER WHEEL.

"A cylinder reputed to contain rolls of paper closely covered with the mystic utterance, weighing 4,000 lb.

severance, worthy of a better cause, with which old men and women may be seen turning these huge cylinders on their pivots through the long hours from dawn to dusk—and to what end? To the ultimate end that all conscious existence may cease.

The determination to ensure the repetition to infinity of this amazing formula obsesses the minds of an entire people. I have seen a prayer cylinder which was reputed to contain rolls of paper closely covered with the mystic utterance, weighing 4000 pounds. No one had ever counted the number of times the sentence was actually inscribed on this vast volume of material, but when it is remembered that a single complete revolution of the cylinder, indicated mechanically by the stroke of a bell, is equivalent to the repetition of the prayer the number of times it is actually inscribed in it; that a devotee turning it produces a complete revolution about once a second, and that the work of turning it proceeds hour after hour, it may be conceded that the number of prayers emitted by such a machine alone, in the course of a single day, is altogether beyond computation. I doubt if there is a monastery in Sikhim which does not possess one or more of these monster cylinders, either in the vestibule to the Lha-khang or in a separate building devoted exclusively to their use. At some monasteries I have seen whole rows of smaller cylinders, running at the height of a man's shoulder, the length of the building's walls, so that he who passed by might turn them on his way. In the Chumbi valley in Tibet, and again at Yuk-sam, the last inhabited spot on the slopes of Kanchenjunga, and on the steep mountain-side above Dentam in Sikhim, I have seen prayer cylinders fitted with water-wheels and revolved without intermission, by the water of unconscious but efficacious mountain streams. Truly the "vain repetitions" of the Pharisees pale into insignificance before this prodigious outpouring. And yet these hill folk are a happy people, always ready to laugh and joke, presenting a striking contrast to the doleful inhabitants of the plains—a fact which should provide material of interest for the psychologist who would investigate the true sources of happiness in the human race.

Before leaving Tashiding we were shown the specialities of the gompa. The largest of the picturesque group of chortens rising in geometrical outline at one end of the enclosure, is invested with a special sanctity due to its being the supposed receptacle of a few of the funereal granules of Ö-sung, a mythical Buddha who is alleged by the theologians, to have preceded Gautama Buddha. It is known as *Thong-wa-rang-tö*, or "Saviour by mere sight," so called on account of the belief that the mere act of beholding it cleanses from all sin. Among the treasures in the temple building itself, we were shown a sacred casket stamped with the seal of the Maharaja of Sikhim, and said to contain a bowl of black stone. This bowl—so we were told—is filled with holy water, and the seal is broken yearly on the 15th day of the first month, when seven cups of its contents are taken out and distributed amongst the pilgrims who attend

Plate 10.

THE GREAT CHORTEN AT TASHIDING.

". . . . known as 'Saviour-by-mere-sight' on account of the belief that the mere act of beholding it cleanses from all sin."

the ceremony. The bowl is then filled up again and sealed for another year.

Before leaving we partook of the salt and greasy tea beloved of Tibet, and then, bidding farewell to the kindly and genial lamas, dropped with a suddenness equal to that of our descent in the morning, to the valley of the Rathong. As we climbed through the lengthening shadows, making our way laboriously up the steep ascent which stretched away between us and our night's resting-place, I looked back across the widening gulf to Tashiding; and it seemed to me that these leisured monks, living aloof from man and close to nature, had developed a wonderfully happy turn for apt nomenclature. The gompa standing in unchallenged isolation upon its wooded height, its white buildings lit up by the slanting rays of the setting sun, was undoubtedly worthy of its name—"the elevated central glory."

From what has been written above it will be seen how far the Buddhism of these mountain lands has parted from the doctrine of the Thera Vada. A departure from the pure intellectualism of the latter made its appearance at a very early date in India itself, and for a proper appreciation of the process by which so great a change was ultimately accomplished, one must take a glimpse at events in the ancient kingdom of Magadha, whence sallied forth the missionaries who carried the doctrine to Tibet in the seventh and eighth centuries A.D.

CHAPTER X

RAJAGRIHA—THE KING'S HOUSE

THE district of Patna, now included in the province of Bihar and Orissa, is rich in archaeological remains spread like a palimpsest over the land, half hiding and half disclosing, vanished pages in the but partly-written book of Indian history. At Rajagriha, for example, one may stand upon the stony hills which once encircled the buildings of a famous city and gaze back, as through a glass darkly, down the chequered flights of time, to a day five centuries before our era, when Bimbisara reigned in Magadha and Gautama preached the excellent law for the salvation of mankind.

It is probable that here we are standing on the site of an even more ancient city, the stronghold of Jarasandha, king of Magadha, nearly a thousand years before the reign of Bimbisara, a warrior who figures prominently in the great war which forms the subject matter of the *Mahabharata*. This, however, must remain a matter of surmise. The ruins of massive fortifications which were certainly built before the days of Bimbisara, lie there before our eyes. But we can only assign them vaguely, as Sir John

Marshall has pointed out, "to some uncertain age before the dawn of history, and rank them, as their stupendousness entitles them to be ranked, among the greatest wonders which primeval man has bequeathed to us." [1]

With the advent of Bimbisara about the time when Nabonidus reigned in Babylon, we emerge from the mists in which the doings of the men of those earlier ages are wrapped, and of the city of his day we can speak with comparative confidence. From the Chinese pilgrim Hiuen Tsiang, who visited the spot during the first half of the seventh century A.D., we learn that it was the central point of the kingdom of Magadha, where the former kings of the country fixed their capital, and that, owing to its producing much of "the most excellent, scented, fortunate grass," it was called Kusagara-pura, "the city of the superior grass." It was also known as Girivraja, "the hill-encircled," and as Rajagriha, "the king's house." The city of Bimbisara was actually deserted before the death of Buddha, probably on account of plague or fire, and a new city built beyond the hills to the north, which also bore the name of Rajagriha.

The ruins of Kusagara-pura which first attract thc attention of the visitor, however, are a legacy from those earlier days of which I have spoken. The remains of massive walls made of large blocks of undressed stone varying in length from three to five feet, and still rising in places to a height of nearly twelve feet, can be seen worming

[1] *Annual Report of the Archaeological Survey of India for the Year 1905–1906.*

their way along the hills which surrounded the city. And at one point, overlooking the low pass which gave access from the hill-girdled city to the plains beyond, still stands an ancient watch-tower of massive undressed stone—the oldest datable building in India. This is, indeed, the famous Pippala stone house of the Chinese pilgrims, where, according to Fa-Hian, who visited the spot somewhere about A.D. 400, Buddha was accustomed to sit in meditation after his mid-day meal. If one approaches it from the pass, one comes, after a brief ascent, to a number of natural hot springs described by the Chinese travellers, around which a group of modern temples has sprung up forming a noted centre of present-day pilgrimage. At no great distance above the springs stands the watch-tower, presenting the appearance of a solid defence work of loosely-bonded roughly-hewn stone. Its present height is approximately 26 feet, and the platform which now forms its summit measures 81 feet by 78 feet. At the foot of the plinth a number of low apertures give access to small chambers in the base of the building. How long before the days of Buddha it was constructed, it is impossible to say; but if the theory which has been put forward, namely, that the chambers referred to were originally used as shelters for the guards, is correct, it is probable that it dates back for a considerable period, since there can be little doubt that it was these chambers that, at the time of King Bimbisara, were used by Buddha and other ascetics as cells in which to meditate. And if this supposition be accepted, it must be assumed that they had long since ceased to play a part in any general scheme of defence.

Behind the stone building is a cave in the hill-side, and of this it was said in the days of Hiuen Tsiang, that it was the abode of notorious Asuras. Strange forms as of Nagas, serpents, and lions were in the habit of issuing from it, and those who had the misfortune to encounter them were apt to lose their reason. Yet so potent was the spell left by the presence of Buddha, that this wonderful place—to quote the book of Hiuen Tsiang—"is one in which holy saints dwell, and occupying the spot consecrated by such sacred traces they forget the calamities and evils that threaten them."[1]

It was from this spot, seated upon the actual handiwork of men who had lived and died at least two and a half millenniums before, that I gazed on a bright December day over the dusty countryside. It wore the empty appearance of a disused theatre; yet its fascination was due to its having provided the stage for a drama of absorbing interest, which was played out during the closing years of the life of Buddha and the opening years of the period immediately following his attainment of Nirvana, which witnessed the early efforts of his disciples at the formation of a Buddhist church. And if such ruins as catch the eye to-day are for the most part legacies from King Jarasandha rather than from King Bimbisara, this was not always so. In the days of the Chinese pilgrims these stony hill-sides still echoed with memories of the Lord Buddha.

[1] *Buddhist Records of the Western World.*

Stupas marking the sites of various incidents in the later years of the sage's mission, were then to be seen in all directions, and were duly catalogued and commented on by the pilgrims in their writings. Buddha himself is represented as speaking with enthusiasm of the various places in or near the city which he frequented. "How pleasant, Ananda, is Rajagriha; how pleasant the Vulture's Peak; how pleasant the Banyan tree of Gotama; how pleasant the Robbers' Cliff; how pleasant the Sathapanni Cave on the slopes of Mount Vebhara; how pleasant the Black Rock on the slope of Mount Isigili; how pleasant the mountain cave of the Serpent's pool in the Sitavana grove; how pleasant the tapoda grove; how pleasant the squirrels' feeding-ground in the bamboo grove; how pleasant Jivaka's mango grove; how pleasant the deer forest of Maddakucchi!"[1] And the chronicler of the travels of Fa-Hian tells how the latter, arming himself with flowers, incense, oil, and lamps, scaled the slopes of the Vulture's Peak, the loftiest of the five mountains surrounding the town, to worship at a retreat frequented by Buddha for purposes of meditation. Fa-Hian ascending the mountain made his offerings and, deeply moved, was scarcely able to restrain his tears as he exclaimed: "Here it was in bygone days Buddha dwelt and delivered the Surangana Sutra. Fa-Hian, not privileged to be born when Buddha lived, can but gaze on the traces of his presence and the place which he occupied."

[1] *Book of the Great Decease*, translated by T. W. and C. A. F. Rhys Davids.

Among the stupas enumerated by Hiuen Tsiang is one built by King Ajatasatru, who succeeded Bimbisara, to the east of the bamboo garden in which Buddha dwelt while in Rajagriha. This, we are told, was built by Ajatasatru to contain the share of the relics of the Exalted One allotted to him, as already narrated. And in this connection I am tempted to make a digression by relating the recent history of another of the eight portions into which the funeral ashes of Buddha are said to have been divided.

* * * * * *

There is in the Presidency of Madras a small village not far from the Kistna river called Bhattiprolu, standing in the centre of a tract of country overspread with ancient monuments in brick and marble. So little respect had the people of the locality for these silent witnesses of a long forgotten age, that they treated them merely as a convenient source on which to draw for material for road-making and other secular purposes, until these acts of vandalism attracted the attention of the authorities.

The interest of the Archaeological Department once aroused, a careful examination of the site was carried out by Mr. Rae, an officer of the department, in 1892. The investigation was rich in results, amongst the finds being three caskets, two of which contained crystal phials in which were enshrined relics of the Buddha with inscriptions to that effect. There are grounds for supposing that these sacred relics were deposited in the stupa of Bhattiprolu at least twenty-one centuries ago, and that they fell to the lot of one of the eight kings, amongst whom the cremation ashes of the great teacher are said to have been distributed. For some years the casket with its precious burden rested in the Madras museum. The Government of India then made it known that they were willing to hand the relic over to any society of Buddhists, which might be in a position to offer it a suitable resting-place. The Mahabodhi Society, under the inspiration of one of its office-bearers, the venerable the Anagarika Dharmapala, accepted the offer; and in due course a vihara for its reception was erected in College Square, Calcutta, under the title of the Sri Dharma Rajika Chaitya Vihara.

It fell to my lot to present the relic to the Society; and on November the 26th, 1920, being the day of the full moon, the ceremony took place. At eight in the morning a great procession of shaven and long-robed monks, nearly half a mile in length, wound its way through the northern gateway into the grounds of Government House, and moving rhythmically to the clash of cymbals and the blare of trumpets, came to the great stone stairway at the northern entrance. At the head of the procession were three Buddhists in pure white robes, bearing upon their shoulders brazen vessels containing holy water from the Ganges. A group of trumpeters followed, and behind them streamed yellow-clad monks from Ceylon, magenta-robed and picturesquely mitred priests from the far Himalayas, detachments from the monasteries of Burma, Siam, China, and Japan. Prominent among those taking part in the proceedings were

Plate 11.

A DEALER IN CHARMS AND SPELLS.

four persons all remarkable in their way—the Hon. Justice Sir Asutosh Mukherjee, C.S.I., President of the Society, the Venerable the Anagarika Dharmapala in flowing robes of crimson silk, a Singalese chief who claimed descent from a contemporary of the Emperor Asoka, and, white-robed and bare-footed, representing the Theosophical Church, the arresting figure of Mrs. Annie Besant. After receiving the relic the procession moved off to the new vihara in College Square, to which I myself proceeded later in the day to take part in the ceremony of consecration.

The ceremony was carried out in strict accordance with ancient Buddhist tradition, which demanded on such occasions, that the king or his representative should first enter the new building unaccompanied, to receive the special blessing of the officiating priests before admission was granted to others. I accordingly unlocked the gate at the entrance and, proceeding alone to the upper story of the building, found myself in the temple, a rectangular hall the walls and ceiling of which were adorned with frescoes copied from the famous paintings at Ajanta. At the far end was an altar, and behind this a stupa six feet or more in height. The temple was empty save for a small number of yellow-robed priests grouped round the stupa, who chanted a blessing in Pali. At the conclusion of this all others taking part in the ceremony were admitted. A further recitation in Pali was given, and the service concluded with short addresses by those chiefly concerned.

So, after the lapse of many centuries, did the ashes of the great teacher find a resting-place in the land watered by the holy river, on whose banks the seed of his teaching had first been sown.

* * * * * *

To return to Rajagriha and the events immediately succeeding the death of Buddha. As already stated, it was in the Sāl grove of the Mallas of Kusinara, a village 140 miles N.N.W. of Rajagriha in a direct line, that the Tatāghata entered into Nirvana. But it was at Rajagriha in a large stone house in the heart of a great bamboo forest, "about five or six *li* on the north side of the southern mountain," that the first Buddhist Council is said to have been held, at the bidding of the venerable Kasyapa after news of the event had been received. "The sun of wisdom has quenched his rays. The world is now in darkness. The illustrious guide has left us and gone, and all flesh must fall into calamity," he exclaimed. And he then reflected: "To secure obedience to the teaching of Buddha we ought to collect the *Dharma-pitaka*," and sounding the great gong he cried: "Now then in the town of Rajagriha there is going to be a religious assembly."[1]

The proceedings of Kasyapa's Council, which is said to have achieved the collection of the *Tripitaka* consisting of the *Sutra-pitaka*, the *Vinaya-pitaka*, and the *Abhidharma-pitaka*, as also of a rival council known as "the assembly of the great congregation" which sat about the

[1] *Buddhist Records of the Western World.*

same time at a spot twenty *li* distant, and added two *pitakas* to the orthodox collection, are described in some detail by the Chinese travellers. These latter, however, were writing more than a thousand years after the events which they were recording, and the prominence given to the story of Ananda's miraculous entrance to the Council of Kasyapa through a closed door, is in itself sufficient to deprive these records of any claim to historical accuracy. They are of interest as establishing the fact that the stories of the miraculous which have been woven into the life of Buddha, had long since established themselves firmly in the Buddhist tradition; and they apprise us, consequently, of the intellectual environment amid which flourished the great centre of Buddhist teaching which sent forth missionaries to carry the doctrine into those lands with which I am now concerned. This was the famous university of Nalanda, which lies buried beneath mounds of earth and debris seven miles north of Rajagriha.

CHAPTER XI

NALANDA—A GREAT UNIVERSITY

IN a Life of Hiuen Tsiang by the Shaman Hwui Li entitled *A History of the Master of the Law of the Three Pitakas of the Great Loving-Kindness Temple*, it is stated baldly, but quite definitely, that after the Nirvana of Buddha a former king called Sakraditya, from a principle of loving obedience to Buddha, built this convent. Two other statements equally explicit, bearing upon the history of Nalanda, appear in the same work. The first is, that six kings in connected succession added to these structures; and the second is, that the priests dwelling at the university were naturally dignified and grave, so that *during the seven hundred years since the foundation of the establishment* there had been no case of rebellion against the rules.

It is clear from these statements that the Chinese pilgrims of the seventh century A.D. were troubled with no doubts as to the history of the origin and rise of Nalanda. So far as they were concerned it was founded by King Sakraditya during the first century B.C., and the work of construction was carried on during six successive reigns. Expert opinion of the present day is not so easily satisfied. The nature of the small finds, and notably of a series of carved panels which now surround the plinth of an ancient temple standing to the east of the main structures, suggests the Gupta period. And the fact that no mention of any university in this neighbourhood is made by Fa-Hian (A.D. 400), while a lengthy description of it is given by Hiuen Tsiang (A.D. 629), has given rise to the suggestion that it was not founded before the middle of the fifth century A.D.

Since the days of Hiuen Tsiang, the hand of time has been busy obliterating the handiwork of man. The methods which she has employed here are identical with those by which she has put away and hidden from sight, the famous cities of Nineveh and Babylon. The traveller, familiar with the dusty mounds dotted over the plains of Assyria and Chaldaea indicating the sites of ancient cities, finds his curiosity aroused as soon as he comes upon the long line of hillocks, stretching north and south for a distance of 1000 yards in the neighbourhood of the modern village of Bargaon. The configuration of the series of mounds indicates two parallel lines of buildings; and the excavations so far undertaken show that the buildings on the east, were the monasteries where the inmates lived and the work of the university was carried on, while those on the west were stupas of considerable size and elaborate design. That upon which the work of excavation has been begun shows successive periods of accretion, the innermost structure being the first, and this having during succeeding periods been encased in others.

At the time of my visit in 1920 the work of excavation had penetrated to what was probably the core of the building, a structure with angle towers and finely preserved sculptuary. All round were numbers of small stupas, and some fine images carved in black basalt had been laid bare. A trench driven for 1500 feet down the line of stupas embraced five of the eight buildings of this character spoken of by Hiuen Tsiang, and showed the intervening spaces covered with numerous smaller structures. The smaller finds included quantities of images varying in size from a few inches to several feet in height, seals and utensils in stone, bronze, copper, pottery, and paste.

The monastery standing a few yards to the east of this stupa—one of a series of nine similar buildings according to Hiuen Tsiang—gives indications of at least five successive structures, each raised upon the foundations of that which preceded it. The main structure of brick with paved courtyards, is a large rectangular building 203 feet east and west by 168 feet north and south. Lines of cells—the residence doubtless of the inmates—open inwards on to a verandah, and this in its turn opens on to a stately courtyard. At one time stone columns, forming the inner line of the verandah, must have constituted a splendid colonnade; and beautiful examples of statuary which have been found *in situ* give some idea of the character of the building. On the northern side of the central courtyard are two cells fashioned to represent caves hewn out of a mountain-side, used, in all probability, for purposes of meditation.

With these striking evidences of past grandeur before one's eyes, one turns with interest, in one's endeavour to reconstruct this amazing institution with its 10,000 inhabitants, to the description of the great university as it was in the seventh century, given in the Life of Hiuen Tsiang. All the more so, in that the Chinese travellers were not here relying upon hearsay or tradition, but were writing of what they themselves saw. The most detailed description of the buildings is that given by the Shaman Hwui Li in his Life of Hiuen Tsiang. From this it would seem that the whole of the buildings stood in a vast enclosure surrounded by a brick wall. Within this enclosure we read of a great college and eight other halls. Curiosity as to the appearance of this striking collection of buildings is piqued by a description which, even if some allowance must be made for the well-known love of Eastern writers for hyperbole, is at least highly suggestive. "The richly adorned towers and the fairy-like turrets, like pointed hill-tops, are congregated together." Actual structural details are then given. "All the outside courts in which are the priests' chambers are of four stages. The stages have dragon projections and coloured eaves, the pearl-red pillars carved and ornamented, the richly adorned balustrades and the roofs covered with tiles that reflect the light in a thousand shades, these things add to the beauty of the scene." A piquant description, and one whose accuracy we have no reason to doubt.

When, however, we come to the account of the impression which these buildings left upon the minds of those who saw them there is greater room for possible exaggeration. "The observatories," declares the enthusiastic Shaman, "seem to be lost in the vapours of the morning, and the upper rooms tower above the clouds. From the windows one may see how the winds and the clouds produce new forms, and above the soaring eaves the conjunctions of the sun and moon may be observed." A poetic description of the landscape completes the picture. "And then we may add how the deep translucent ponds bear on their surface the blue lotus, intermingled with the Kie-ni (*Butea frondosa*) flowers, of deep red colour, and at intervals the Amra groves spread over all their shade." After this it is not surprising to learn that, "while the Sangharamas of India are counted by myriads, this is the most remarkable for grandeur and height."

Such was the university of Nalanda to which in or about the year A.D. 632 came Hiuen Tsiang. To gain admission a man must have studied deeply books both old and new; and the tests imposed were so severe that though learned men flocked to its doors from different cities, those who failed compared with those who succeeded, were "as seven or eight to ten."[1] The day, we are told, was not sufficient for asking and answering profound questions, and from morning to night they engaged in discussion. The 10,000 inmates all studied the Great Vehicle, from which it is clear that it was a great centre of Mahayāna Buddhism; but even so, the curriculum was by no means confined to the Buddhist Canon. The

[1] *Buddhist Records of the Western World.*

Plate 12.

THE ALTAR OF A CHAPEL IN BHUTAN.

Samkhya system and works on magic are specifically mentioned by Hwui Li, and Hiuen Tsiang states in particular that he had come to Nalanda to be instructed in the principles of the Yoga-Sastra. During his five years' residence he heard the explanation of the Yoga-Sastra three times; and a list of other works to which he devoted himself in addition to the Buddhist Canon, is given in his biography by Hwui Li.

With this graphic picture of the intellectual atmosphere of the great Buddhist university before us, we are in a position to appreciate the change which had already been brought about in the character of Buddhist thought, since the early days when the Elders of the order had drawn up the doctrine of the Thera Vada. These changes continued and resulted eventually in the disappearance of Buddhism from the plains of India. They are of sufficient importance, therefore, to merit further examination.

CHAPTER XII

THE FATE OF INDIAN BUDDHISM

ANY attempt to trace in detail the various causes which contributed towards the disappearance of Buddhism from the land of its birth, would require far greater space than could be appropriately devoted to the subject in the present volume. The main cause, and the one which is relevant to my present theme, was undoubtedly the change in its own nature brought about by its attempt to absorb other beliefs and practices with which it came in contact. The teaching of the Mahayāna school itself constituted a wide departure from that of the Thera Vada. The latter appealed to the intellect—salvation was to be obtained by knowledge ; the former ministered to the emotions—salvation could be obtained by faith and worship. The one was rationalistic and atheistic ; the other developed a mystic theology. It followed that the Thera Vada was exclusive, while the Mahayāna was popular. And above all, the adherents of the Mahayāna concerned themselves with the mystery of the hereafter which Buddha himself consistently refused to discuss.

The tendency to depart from this injunction of Gautama displayed itself in very early days. It is recorded of King Pasenadi of Kosala, a contemporary of King Bimbisara and his successor King Ajatasatru of Magadha, that encountering the nun Khenia shortly after the death of Buddha he asked her: "Does the Perfect One exist after death?" And that at the conclusion of the dialogue which followed, the latter declared: "Released, O great king, is the Perfect One from this, that his being should be gauged by the measure of the corporeal world: he is deep, immeasurable, unfathomable as the great ocean." Here at least is no denial of a hereafter. Such tendencies developed further about the time of the Council said to have been held at Vesali, a century after the death of Buddha. They took more definite shape in the reign of King Kanishka during the second century A.D., and attained a high state of development under the inspiration of teachers like Nagarjuna at the end of the second century A.D. and Asvaghosa about the fifth century.

It is claimed by a Buddhist writer of the present day that the Mahayānist doctrine is not a departure from the teaching of Buddha, but a development of it. His contention is that in original Buddhism, by which he means the teaching of the Thera Vada, Buddha has confined himself to an explanation of the external world, leaving aside the question of the nature of the real that lies behind the apparent; or, in other words, "his main subject was Phenomenology and not Ontology, though from his own point of view he at once understood the true perception after having obtained Enlightenment."[1]

It is the latter aspect of Buddha's knowledge that forms the chief subject of the Mahayānist doctrine—that which lies beyond or behind the phenomenal world, that of which we can only say with certainty that it is beyond the law of causality. And according to Mr. Kimura the Mahayānist theory of ultimate reality is indistinguishable from the absolutism of the monistic Vedantists: "In Mahayāna Buddhism all individual beings are identified with the 'Mahatma,' *i.e.* the absolute ego. . . . Their sense of 'Mahatma' is not different from that of 'Nirguna Brahma' of Vedanta."[2] Once it was admitted that consideration of such problems was a legitimate function of Buddhism, speculation ran riot. The Chinese traveller Fa-Hian, writing of his experiences in India about the year A.D. 400, tells us that "men attached to the Mahayāna" made offerings to "Prajnaparamita," a mystical treatise produced by Nagarjuna and attributed by him to Gautama himself, and to "Manjusri and Avalokitesvara." Manjusri crystallised into the god of Wisdom, and as such occupies a high position in the pantheon of present-day Lamaism. Avalokitesvara was accorded an important place in the scheme of *dhyani* Buddhas, one of the most fanciful, surely, of all the ideas evolved by the Mahayānist theologians. The *dhyani* Buddha is a mystical being dwelling in some transcendental habitat

[1] R. Kimura in vol. iv. of the *Journal of the Department of Letters*, published by the Calcutta University. [2] *Ibid.*

beyond the material universe. Each *dhyani* Buddha has two counterparts, a human Buddha and a Bodhisatwa, the latter being a potential Buddha. Five of these somewhat unintelligible trinities are regarded as appertaining to the present *kalpa* (aeon), the most important being naturally the one in which Gautama plays the part of the earthly Buddha. In this particular trinity the *dhyani* Buddha is Amitabha, and the Bodhisatwa, Avalokiteswara. In the Tibetan manuscript entitled the *Mani-kah-bum* it is related that "once upon a time Amitabha, after giving himself up to earnest meditation, caused a white ray of light to issue from his right eye which brought Padmapani (Avalokiteswara) into existence." It is further stated that Amitabha blessed his offspring, whereupon the Bodhisatwa brought forth the mystic words, "Om mani padme, hum!"

Buddhism had in fact reached a stage when it was prepared to admit almost any god to its pantheon and any doctrine to its rapidly expanding theology: a state of affairs which has evoked the caustic comment of Professor Rhys Davids that "under the overpowering influence of these sickly imaginings . . . the whole sky was filled with forgeries of the brain, and the nobler and simpler lessons of the founder of the religion were smothered beneath the glittering mass of metaphysical subtleties."[1]

This very catholicity which made Mahayāna Buddhism popular possessed the seeds of its decay. The beliefs and practices which it

[1] *Buddhism*, by T. W. Rhys Davids.

attempted to absorb flourished within its tolerant embrace. The influence which Hinduism exerted upon it increased with the Brahmanical revival which took place during the Gupta period. Nalanda, as we have seen—the Oxford of Buddhist India—was not merely a great centre of Mahayānist Buddhism in the seventh century A.D., but was interested profoundly in other doctrines.

Still, its reputation as an intellectual centre was high. Its head, at the time of Hiuen Tsiang's visit, was a famous scholar, Silabhadra, of whom it has been said that there have been few scholars versed to an equal extent in all the shastras. And the standard of morality was still unimpaired. Yet among the scholars of Nalanda itself there were already forebodings. In a conversation with Silabhadra while he was yet a student, his guru Dharmapala, then head of the Buddhist organisation, is reported to have said, "The glory of Buddhism is on the wane. Irreligion is spreading among us like a cloud. Unless we succeed in scattering it, there is no hope for the progress of Buddhism."[1] His fears were only too well founded. The black arts, including magic and sorcery, crept in.

Gradually the fears with which Buddha himself is said to have been assailed when, much against his will, he was persuaded to admit women to the order, were realised. "If, Ananda, in the doctrine and the order which the Perfect One has founded it were not conceded to women

[1] See an article by Mahamahopadhyaya Hara Prasad Shastri contributed to the *Journal of the Bihar and Orissa Research Society* for December 1919.

to go out from their homes into homelessness, holy living would remain preserved, Ananda, for a long time. . . . But now, Ananda, that in the doctrine and order which the Perfect One has founded women renounce the world and go into homelessness, under these circumstances, Ananda, holy living will not be long preserved."[1]

A volume of Buddhist hymns found in the royal library at Khatmandu has recently been published by Mahamahopadhyaya Hara Prasad Shastri. "Of the subject matter of these *dohas*," the Mahamahopadhyaya writes, "the less said the better. They belong to a period when the Buddhist wise men wanted to show an easy entrance to Nirvana through sensual enjoyments, which is still the burden of many extant religious sects of India."

The collection, under the title of *Charyagiti*, is made up of the songs of twenty different authors who lived in all probability during the tenth century A.D. It bears witness to the development at that time of a strong vernacular Buddhist literature, which exerted a marked influence upon Tibetan religious thought. It also throws a flood of light upon the demoralisation which the religious thought of the times had already undergone. It is typical of a literature which came into existence, the product of a destructive wave of eroticism which swept over the land, invading Buddhism and Hinduism alike. The practices inculcated in such works seem to have been prevalent in Buddhism by the tenth century. In Hinduism they were

[1] *Buddha*, by H. Oldenberg.

associated with the cult of Shiva, and from the Shivaits they spread to the worshippers of Vishnu also. And an aftermath of this era of sexual exaltation is to be found even at the present day in certain of the rites of a certain school of Shaktas, as well as in the still more obscure ritual of the modern adherents of the cult of Sahajia.

Much might be written on this subject; but my object is merely to show that, following the adoption of such ideas and practices, a period of moral degeneration set in during which Buddhism became wholly disintegrated. And when a revival again took place it was Hinduism which rose from the pit in which Indian Buddhism had died. The devouring sword of Islam may have hastened the end; but what the Muhammadan found to destroy was but the husk from which the kernel had already gone.

And if further evidence be required of the main cause of the disappearance of Buddhism from Bengal, it is to be found in the discoveries which have been made in recent years, of the existence there at the present day of a peculiar type of worship known as Dharma-worship. This had been identified by Rai Dinesh Chandra Sen Bahadur and by Mahamahopadhyaya Hara Prasad Shastri, among other investigators, as the direct though degenerate descendant of Buddhism. The arguments in support of this contention are set forth by the Mahamahopadhyaya in a monograph entitled the *Discovery of Living Buddhism in Bengal*, published by the Sanskrit Press Depository in Calcutta in 1897, and are too long to be summarised here. The conclusion arrived at has been confirmed by subsequent investigations and may be stated briefly as follows. Dharma Thakur, the chief object of worship in this curious and little-known creed, is derived from Dharma, the doctrine which formed the central conception of the Buddhist creed. The ceremony of initiation into Buddhism included the repetition by the candidate of the following formula: "I take my refuge in the Buddha; I take my refuge in the Doctrine (Dharma); I take my refuge in the Order (Sangha)." By a process of anthropomorphism the Dharma of this trinity has become Dharma Thakur, a divinity taking a place, albeit the highest, in a pantheon consisting largely of Hindu deities. In a temple of Dharma in Calcutta, for example, the Mahamahopadhyaya found five prominent images in addition to that of Dharma, namely, Ganesh, Panchanand, Shitala the goddess of smallpox, Sasthi the goddess of procreation, and Jvarasura the demon of fever. The cult is confined to the lowest classes of so-called Hindus, and its priests are drawn from the lowest castes. Its formulae are in ungrammatical Bengali and equally ungrammatical Sanskrit, and the ritual includes the sacrifice of animals before the deity. Both its theory and its practice are as the poles asunder from those of early Buddhism; and nothing short of the perseverance and ingenuity of those who have investigated it could have served to show a connection between the two.

From this brief survey it will be seen that the

process of decay was gradual and, as has been shown, had set in, though it had not reached a malignant stage, at the time of Hiuen Tsiang's visit to Nalanda in the seventh century A.D. If the standard of learning at that time was high, it flourished nevertheless in an atmosphere of credulity. Stories of supernatural events were current in the university itself, and on all sides monuments in the shape of stupas marked the scenes of miraculous happenings in the Buddha's life. The soil was clearly one in which occultism would be likely to flourish, and it is probable that from the seventh century onwards a tendency towards a highly ritualistic form of Buddhism, to which the term "Tantṛik" is commonly applied, rapidly gathered strength.

Such was the state of affairs when, among those who came to Nalanda from distant lands, was one Guru Padma-sambhava, a priest well versed in the lore of the Tantrik Yogacarya School of Buddhism. He came from the country of Udyana, situated in the far north-west among the rugged mountains south of the Hindu Kush, a land famous for the proficiency of its priests in necromancy. He must have reached Nalanda during the first half of the eighth century A.D., and somewhere about the year A.D. 747, at the invitation of King Thi-Sron Detsan, proceeded to Tibet. Here under the title of Guru Rim-po-ché he laid the foundations of the strange religion which one finds widespread over the eastern Himalayas at the present day.

The story of his birth prevalent in Tibet is in keeping with the creed of mystery and magic

Plate 13.

A PRAYER WHEEL DRIVEN BY WATER.

which he propagated. It was preceded by a period of mourning in the kingdom of Udayana caused by the death of the king's son. The offerings and prayers of the people rising from this land of woe reached the heaven of Amitabha and met with a speedy answer. Like the sovereign of another ancient land, the king of Udayana dreamed dreams. And in the visions of the night he saw himself glorious and refulgent, the wielder of a golden thunderbolt. Such a dream could portend nothing but good fortune, and he had not to wait for the interpretation thereof. The very next morning news was brought to him, by the priest of the royal household, that an unearthly light was shining upon the Dhanakosha lake. The king hurried to the scene, and embarking upon the waters of the lake found, seated upon a lotus flower of matchless beauty, a handsome boy sceptered and shining like a god. Bowing down before him he questioned him and was told :

"I come in accordance with the prophecy of the great Sakya Muni who said, 'Twelve hundred years after me, in the north-east of the Udyana country, in the pure lake of Kosha, a person more famed than myself will be born and be known as Padma-sambhava or the lotus-born, and he shall be the teacher of my esoteric mantra doctrine and shall deliver all beings from misery.'"[1]

There is no need to dwell upon the influence which this happy event had upon the fortunes of Udayana. All that concerns us here is that

[1] *The Buddhism of Tibet*, by L. A. Waddell.

after many wanderings the Guru, as already stated, found his way to Nalanda and thence to Tibet, where with his thunderbolt—the "vajra" of India and the "dorje" of Tibet—and his mantras he vanquished—so one is told to-day—the demons that haunted the land, and laid firm the foundations upon which have been built up the elaborate edifice of present-day Lamaism.

What he actually did was undoubtedly to compromise with the demon-worship which he found rampant throughout the land, by admitting a prodigious host of spirits, both malignant and benign, into an already overcrowded pantheon.

What wonder, then, if the result to-day is a perfectly bewildering medley of gods and goddesses, buddhas and bodhisatwas, guardian deities and canonised saints, ghouls, goblins and demons, deified kings and spirits of every conceivable description, paradises, earths and hells?

Yet despite the vast gulf which separates twentieth-century Lamaism from the teaching of the princely Sage, who made the great renunciation that he might find salvation for mankind more than two thousand five hundred years ago, there are among lamas and laymen alike an attractive gentleness and kindliness of disposition, a dignified and courteous hospitality, and withal a cheerfulness and friendliness, which bear witness that the influence of an outstanding character and personality lives and works for good, unaffected by the flight of time.

CHAPTER XIII

THE ROAD TO CHUMBI

It was in the Earth-horse year of the fifteenth cycle of the Tibetan almanac, corresponding to the year A.D. 1918 of the less imaginative Gregorian calendar, that I crossed the dividing line between Sikhim and Tibet—a feat, as will become apparent shortly, on a par with that of an idol of my childhood's days, one Jack who climbed a beanstalk which towered as high as heaven. True, it was not a giant's castle which awaited us ; yet it was a land where flourished mysteries of as astonishing an order as those which displayed themselves to Jack.

Late in October we had trekked across the thirty odd miles from Darjeeling to Kalimpong, the *entrepôt* of the main Tibetan trade route, down which stream strings of sturdy mules with loads of wool and other merchandise, and the scene of the amazing missionary enterprise which owes its phenomenal success to the ability and zeal of Dr. J. A. Graham and his family. And we had completed there the commissariat and transport arrangements for our journey.

A pleasant walk up the hill-side above the bazaar, through the famous St. Andrew's Colonial

Homes, one of the most remarkable of Dr. Graham's many philanthropic activities, took us a little off our direct route, but compensated us with a magnificent view of all the country drained by the Tista river. Pushing on along a hill-side covered with thick masses of aromatic wormwood, growing to a height of four or five feet, we reached in due course the goal of our first day's march, a cosy bungalow perched in a small clearing on the top of a heavily wooded knoll, 6400 feet above sea-level. From here we gazed back over the tumbled spurs of the outer Himalaya to the plains behind, stretching away till they lost themselves in a distant and shadowy horizon. Time and place cried aloud for an artist. The pink blossoms of a Luculia tree standing ten or twelve feet high waved in at the windows; and a fiery sunset lit up, with great flames of burning crimson, banks of fantastic-shaped clouds that hung heavily over the vast chain of mountains, frowning across at us from the Tibetan borderland.

The next day we dropped down the far side of the ridge on which we had spent the night, thus pulling down a curtain, as it were, between ourselves and the now distant plains. Henceforth the word *plain* was blotted out of our vocabulary, and we struggled valiantly with the terminology of a dialect born and nurtured in a land consecrated to mountains. We descended at first by easy stages from Rississum at 6400 feet through verdant forest to the hamlet of Pedong at 4900 feet, the centre of a cultivated slope; and from here, stimulated by the eerie music wafted to us from an adjacent monastery, much more rapidly and abruptly to the valley of the Rushett Chu, a modest 2000 feet above sea-level. During the remainder of a twelve-mile march we ascended again *via* a small village named Rhenok at 3200 feet to our night's halting-place at Ari, 4700 feet.

The next morning a farther descent awaited us to the Rongli river at 2700 feet. The bean-stalk was yet to climb. It seemed, however, that this time we had indeed reached the foot of it. I craned my head upwards to see the horizon at a preposterous angle; and, less impetuous than Jack, we decided to take it in two stages, and were content with a first stride of something under 4000 feet, which landed us at Sedonchen, 6500 feet.

The second stride, which we took the following day, was a much more serious matter. The weather was wet and misty and, as we discovered later, snow was falling on the crests above us. The track was one of those execrable stone staircases, all slippery knobs and ankle-twisting hollows, which exacerbate the temper of anything except a Tibetan mule, and whose solitary merit is that they resist with partial success the disintegrating proclivities of the Sikhim rains. Indeed there have been occasions—rare perhaps, but actually known to have occurred, as we ourselves can testify—when even the Tibetan mule has been nonplussed by them. The one occasion to which we can bear personal witness occurred on our return journey, when an unwisely meandering animal precipitated the load and (unintentionally, no doubt) itself over an adjacent khud. The Elder, who regards the dispensing of the contents of the travelling medicine chest as his prerogative, had out iodine, ligatures, needles, and other appliances in no time; and with the assistance of the Cavalry Officer, whose aid was called in "to hold the mule steady," sewed up the resulting gashes.

In the space of rather less than nine miles we levered ourselves up a farther 6000 feet, thus bringing us to a height of 12,000 feet, the highest point which, for the time being, it was necessary for us to scale. A wayside tea-shop kept by an enterprising Chinaman and his wife afforded welcome shelter and refreshment. Indeed for us it acquired an almost historic importance, for it was here that the Elder declared that he had reached the stage of being able to drink Tibetan tea "without revulsion." The Cavalry Officer was not quite certain whether this was intended to be taken literally, that is to say, whether the words "without revulsion" applied to the tea itself or merely to the Elder's feelings.

There is, a little above the track, a peak of historic interest and of supreme beauty, and since we were tempted to make a diversion in its favour on the return journey, a reference may be made to it now.

Away to the north the dry highlands of Tibet shimmered in the sun under a cloudless sky. In front of us—we were then, of course, approaching the peak from the Tibetan side—dense banks of clouds rested on the southern ranges, and lay piled up like giant stacks of cotton-wool in many of the valleys. To our right, the pure white peaks of the Kanchenjunga group rose from a rolling mass of grey and white cloud which blocked out all view of the valleys and lower hills, into a vast void of blue. To our left the rugged outline of Gyi-mo-chi, the meeting-place of Sikhim, Bhutan, and Tibet, showed fitfully through drifting curtains of mist. On a convenient site provided by a small hump projecting a little below the summit of the peak, stood the remains of the old Tibetan fort of Lingtu, straggling structures of unshaped stone now a few feet only in height. From the fort itself the track of a flanking wall running to the crest was still discernible. It was an insignificant structure, yet history had centred round it. For it was Tibetan encroachment here that led to the brief expedition into Tibet of 1888; to the Anglo-Chinese convention concerning Sikhim and Tibet of 1890; and, indirectly, at a later date, to no less an event than the rending of the veil behind which the mystery city of Lhasa had so long lain hid. Thus do small things lead to great. The story can be recalled in a few words.

It was in the autumn of 1886 that a party of Tibetans crossed the Jelap La and dug themselves in—walled themselves in would be the more accurate description—at Lingtu. By so doing they violated the sanctity of Sikhim and challenged our authority as the suzerain power. We referred the matter to the Chinese, and waited patiently for a year for the redress which never came. Then we took action. We wrote a letter to the leader of the raiders ordering the evacuation of Lingtu. This was towards the close of the year 1887. We were precise—almost meticulous—in our language. We said that the evacuation must be effected by the fifteenth day of the following March. And then we waited once more. Immediate developments were not promising. The letter was returned whence it had come—unopened. A representation to the Dalai Lama likewise remained unanswered; and on March the 20th a British force advanced upon Lingtu. The Tibetans retired without fighting, and the punitive force took up a position at Gnatong. Twice more during the year 1888, in May and in September, did the Tibetans return; and twice more were they driven back over the Jelap La.

This seemed to the authorities to be a suitable occasion for setting in motion once more the complex apparatus of diplomacy, and another year of desultory negotiation with the Chinese rolled by. And then an unexpected thing happened—the stock of British patience became exhausted. This not only surprised, but alarmed the Chinese, who, with characteristic perverseness and with an altogether alien alacrity, pressed for a diplomatic settlement of the points at issue. Out of this new-born enthusiasm for agreement came the Anglo-Chinese Convention of 1890 and the subsequent trade regulations of 1893.

So much for the Chinese. But if they were pleased the Tibetans were not. They studiously ignored the provisions of both agreements. And it was ten years of contumacy on their part that decided the Government of Great Britain to deal direct with Tibet, and that led to the now historic mission of Colonel (now Sir F.) Younghusband to Lhasa.

History always acquires a new interest when one visualises the events which it records on the ground on which they were actually staged, and we pondered upon these happenings awhile, as we sat on the ruined walls on the summit of Lingtu. And then we cast our gaze down over the ascent which has been described. And we agreed that, impressive as it had been as we made the ascent, it was even more striking when looked at in reverse. From where we sat the track zigzagged hurriedly down the mountain-side for fifteen miles to Rongli; and during the passage of those memorable fifteen miles, as we were soon to discover, it drops all but 10,000 feet.

On the outward journey we left Lingtu on our right and pushed on, skirting along what may be described as the edge of the roof of Tibet to Gnatong, a bare cup in the mountains in which a collection of wooden huts, dumped down dolefully at an altitude of 12,200 feet, provides shelter for the traveller and others who are eccentric enough to wish to live there — a relic of the Tibetan expedition of 1904. It is on record that during the earlier proceedings of 1888 described above, the Tibetans in the course of a single night constructed a wall above Gnatong, three miles long and three or four feet high. No traces of this remarkable achievement, however, now remain.

From this bleak spot, a considerable effort will

carry one in a day over the frontier and down into the Chumbi valley on the far side—if the word *down* can be used without danger of misunderstanding in the case of a valley the floor of which is 10,000 feet up. A walk of eight miles brings one to the actual boundary line which cuts the track at the summit of the Jelap La, 14,390 feet, the exact point being marked by a cairn of stones from which flutter a vast collection of prayer flags, added to by every pious Buddhist who chances to pass this way. On arrival our head muleteer, Ten Tzing, hastened to put himself right with the Powers of the unseen World by adding his own, secured from, and duly blessed by, the head lama of a monastery in the neighbourhood of Darjeeling, as part of the preparation for the journey. He was then ready to give information about the outstanding features of the landscape, while our teeth chattered in the wind and our feet got numb in a newly-fallen covering of snow.

The arresting feature was the glittering cone of Cho-mo-lhari, which appeared to rise in majestic isolation from a rampart of burnt sienna, cutting in hard outline a wide stretch of the horizon. In reality it stands far behind the chain from which it seems to rise, away to the north of Phari Jong, a splendid pinnacle little short of 24,000 feet. To our right another striking peak, Ma-song-chong-drong-ri, rose above the general level of the surrounding highlands.

Once over the Jelap, we followed the sinuous course of a rugged ravine, by a boulder-strewn track calculated to give the stone staircases of

Sikhim an absurdly high opinion of themselves by comparison. Comments were inevitable; but anything in the nature of a dissertation on road construction in mountain regions, was choked off by the Sardar Bahadur's curt and unanswerable observation that we were in Tibet. This summing up of the situation was accepted as conclusive, and we relapsed into silence. At 4 P.M. the same day, some hours ahead of our transport, we touched New Yatung, the chief village of the Chumbi valley.

* * * * * *

To any one who has followed the chequered history of Tibet during recent years the Chumbi valley tells a graphic story. It is strewn with the material evidences of a recent though evanescent Chinese occupation. Barracks and official residences force themselves upon one's notice, but they stand silent and empty, tombstones upon the grave of a perished cause. Far be it from me to attempt to unravel the tortuous workings of the Chinese official mind. I recount only facts. Whatever the reason, there appeared in Lhasa early in the year 1910, large numbers of Chinese soldiers. Whether by accident or design they came into violent collision with the people of the capital, thus producing a situation which was clearly critical, for the Dalai Lama fled panic-stricken from the Potala, and reached Yatung in time which, I was assured, has never before or since been beaten. Hard on his heels came a posse of Chinese officials. Both sought the good offices of the British assistant trade agent, the shrewd son of a Scotch father and a

Tibetan mother, and the fortunate husband of an admirable Nepali wife. The position was one of some embarrassment. The house of the assistant trade agent was small—obviously never intended for the entertainment of such exalted guests. The embarrassment of the involuntary host was added to, by the insistence of the Chinese upon their being shown into the private presence of the Dalai Lama, and the obstinate refusal of the latter to tolerate them in his sight. Eventually, by arrangement, each Chinese in turn was ushered into the presence by the British representative himself. It cannot be said that this compromise was fruitful of results. The high Pontiff of Tibet preserved a dignified and, as it turned out, a baffling silence; and the spokesmen of China retired one by one discomfited. Moreover, having outstripped their own escort in their hot pursuit, they found themselves unwelcome guests amid a hostile populace, and in their turn sought the good offices of the British representative, who accommodated them in the Dâk Bungalow for the night. The next morning the Dalai Lama left early—and apprehensive—but succeeded in crossing the frontier unmolested, whence he made his way to Kalimpong. Such in brief was the prelude to a three years' sojourn in British territory on the part of the priestly potentate who, by his success in preserving his country in effective isolation from the remainder of the planet, had been responsible for one of the most striking anachronisms of the twentieth century.

Quite recently the Chumbi valley had been the

A man of Chumbi.

scene of yet another migration. The tables had been turned. The Dalai Lama, no longer a refugee, sat once more in the seats of the mighty behind the massive walls of the Potala at Lhasa. Not even the presence of a Chinese amban disturbed the seclusion which once more shrouded the capital from the prying eyes of the outside world. And along the stony passage of the Chumbi valley streamed disarmed Chinese soldiers, seeking the asylum impartially extended by Great Britain to all in need of it. For a time the vanquished Chinese army rested gratefully in a small enclave provided for them at Kalimpong, within sight of the house where, eight years before, the Dalai Lama had halted, and where the rooms which he occupied and the gorgeous priestly furnishings are reverently preserved intact by Tobgay Dorjé, the youthful Prime Minister of Bhutan. And then it passed on back to its own country, leaving behind jetsam in the shape of a few who found the actual conditions of life in Kalimpong, pleasanter than the prospect of a return to the greater uncertainties of life in China. And among them, it is worth recording, an artist whose pictorial genius has already attracted the attention of connoisseurs from Calcutta, and bids fair to excitc interest in still wider circles.

CHAPTER XIV

NECROMANCY

At the head of the Chumbi valley there is a monastery of repute attached to the Geylukpa, or Yellow cap sect, known as the Tung-kar gompa. Attracted by the high reputation for learning enjoyed by the presiding lama, and even more, perhaps, by certain persistent rumours of the presence at the monastery of a mysterious oracle through whom converse might be held with the unseen world, we determined to pay it an early visit, and arranged to devote to the expedition the first day of our brief stay.

There exists in Tibet, however, a somewhat rigid social etiquette, and before a start was possible, the welcome of the head-men of the neighbouring villages claimed our attention. This consisted of offerings—mainly joints of meat, including a somewhat gruesome *pièce de résistance* in the shape of a huge yak's head upon a charger; and in the case of every man, a scarf. Throughout Tibet and the neighbouring countries the presentation of scarves has become a practice from which good manners permit of no departure. The scarves vary in size and material, but except in Mongolia, where they are said to be pale blue, are, in my experience, invariably white. There is an elaborate ritual which provides for the presentation, acceptance, or exchange of scarves on arrival and departure, and prescribes the circumstances under which they shall be kept or returned. Among the scarves which I received was one handed to me on behalf of the Dalai Lama himself. The origin of the custom is shrouded in obscurity; but the researches of the Sardar Bahadur, conducted with the assistance of certain ancient Tibetan manuscripts supplied by the Dalai Lama, are responsible for the hypothesis that the practice arose out of a duel between the supernatural power of a famous priest and the worldly arrogance of an equally famous king.

Srong-tsan-gampo, the ruler of Tibet, heard of the advent of Guru Rimpoché, the Buddhist missionary whose story I have already told, and whose image finds a place above the altar in so many temples at the present day, and jealous of the fame of this Indian preacher, determined that he should make obeisance to him. The priest, divining the haughty spirit of the king, accepted the challenge of temporal to spiritual power, and on entering his presence threw out his arms as though about to bow down before him. But behold a miracle! Tongues of flame shot forth from the priestly fingers, licking the august person of the king, and impregnating with the smell of fire the scarf which he wore. The victory over pride was won. The king humbled himself before this display of miraculous power, and bowing down, offered the priest his scarf in token of humility.

* * * * * *

The sun was well past the meridian when, in company with a motley crowd—shepherds, peasants, muleteers, and lamas—we trooped expectantly from the yard of the main building of the Tung-kar gompa to an adjoining hall. The floor of one half of the hall was raised to form a platform a foot or two above the general level, along the edge of which ran a rail with a break in the centre, resembling the altar rail of an English church. In the centre, in place of an altar, there stood a high and gaudily decorated throne over which was spread a huge golden umbrella. And seated upon the throne was the oracle, robed in gorgeous raiment of brightly flowered silk, while upon his brow rested a fantastic head-dress trimmed with a chaplet of grinning skulls. A circular breastplate of chased metal, recalling irresistibly the Urim and Thummim of a high priest of a bygone age, and a heavy broad-bladed sword, completed his equipment.

The stage was deftly set with a view to creating an atmosphere appropriate to a display of necromancy. Below the platform rails, on our right as we faced the throne, stood a small altar, and here two lamas poured libations and chanted invocations to the deity in a subdued hypnotic monotone, punctuating their prayer from time to time with the shrill clang of a temple bell. On the left other lamas joined in the invocation, adding to their appeal the boom and crash of

Plate 15.

A LAMA MEDIUM.

"Seated on the throne was the oracle robed in gorgeous raiment of brightly flowered silk."

drum and cymbal. During the opening prayers the figure on the throne sat with closed eyes and with body thrown slightly forward. Presently a tremor passed through his body, followed, after a short interval, by a violent oscillation of the legs. The cymbals crashed with increasing violence, and the deep boom of the drum reverberated on the air. The figure, upon which all eyes were now fixed, became rapidly convulsed. The body was thrust forward from the waist and was swept from side to side in spasmodic semicircular motions. Shaken from head to foot, he rose suddenly to his full height and seized from an attendant lama, the broad two-edged sword. This was the signal, apparently, for which all were waiting in hushed expectancy, conveying the information that the spirit had entered into his body and was in full possession.

The crowd of onlookers could no longer restrain their emotion, and rushing forward bowed their heads to the ground in reverent awe. Possessed of the sword the figure resumed his seat upon the throne, and I watched carefully, making notes of what took place. His face assumed a contorted expression, and he soon began gasping horribly, while he choked out in painful spasms a succession of guttural noises. A lama specially trained for the purpose, wrote rapidly as the tormented being jerked out these strange and scarcely articulate utterances, breathing stertorously the while and swaying from side to side in convulsive movement. After a time he rose again, like a man wrestling fiercely with some unseen foe, and then his whole frame wilted, and he fell back limp and motionless as a corpse, propped hideously against the back of the throne.

Were we witnesses of an unintended tragedy ? Had the possessing spirit departed, and in his company had life actually ebbed away ? Such apprehensions were not shared by the officiating lamas, for no sooner had the sudden and, as I had half feared, tragic silence descended upon the scene, than it was broken into by further deep-throated invocations. The medium proved obligingly responsive, and a second possession took place. This time many of the onlookers were completely carried away, crowding round the throne, casting scarves upon the shoulders of its occupant and beseeching his blessing. They received in return charms and pills possessing healing properties. I had an opportunity later of handling these latter, for Ten Tzing was among those who had been thus favoured, and he showed me a small handful of round chocolate-coloured balls, the size of a large pea. These he told me would act as charms so long as he was well and would cure him when he fell ill—a striking combination of properties, though it inconveniently occurred to me that if they were efficacious in their first capacity, it was unnecessary for them to be endowed with their second. At the close of the second possession the medium gradually recovered consciousness.

What was the nature of the phenomenon which we had witnessed ? Was the state into which the subject had been thrown akin to that of epilepsy ? Was it induced by auto-suggestion ? Or was it wholly simulated ? We could come to no certain conclusion. The lama himself assured us that while in the state of trance, he was completely unconscious and retained no recollection of anything that passed. Attention had at first been drawn to him on account of periodic fits of strange behaviour, when he was wont to act as one gone mad. This seemed to support the theory of epilepsy. So marked did his behaviour become that he was sent to Lhasa to be examined. And in due course the wise men of Lhasa declared that the possession was genuine, and an edict went forth that he was the mouthpiece of the gods. And by a process of deduction, the precise nature of which was not disclosed, they arrived at a more particular statement of the case, and declared that the spirit which took possession of him was that of Shong Tön, a celebrated lama of Tashi-lhumpo, who had passed from the earth plane many years before with the vow that, as he had failed to inculcate the masses with the pure doctrine of Buddhism during his lifetime, he would do so after death.

Ten days later I was back in Calcutta, a circumstance which induced certain reflections upon the purely relative nature of time. For ooking back it seemed to me that the oracle of Tung-kar was just as near, or just as far off, as the cave of the witch of Endor.

CHAPTER XV

TO GANGTOK, AND MORE ABOUT LAMAISM

IN Darjeeling the autumn is a period of efflorescence. During September a large flowering tree, the Erythrina, attracts attention, with its blossoms of bright scarlet. A shrub with a little pink flower, the *Osbeckia crinita*, a member of the family known to horticulturists as melastoma, or honey-throat, grows in wild profusion in the woods, while a larger member of the same family with a flower of deep purple may be seen in some of the gardens. By the middle of October the gardens are aflame with the ruddy glow of the scarlet salvia, and the eye is caught in every direction by thickets of pink and white cosmos. Other blossoms that attracted attention as we swung down the steep descent to the Rungeet river on a bright October morning, were those of the hibiscus, painting the dingy background of the forest with patches of glowing crimson.

On the far side of the river we climbed through a belt of Sāl forest, and later ran into a zone of dense undergrowth picked out here and there with clumps of giant bamboo, while for colour there were several varieties of marigold and clusters of delicate little flowers, white, yellow and mauve.

Some miles short of our destination we passed through a hamlet of half-a-dozen Nepali houses with the attractive name of Ki Tam, signifying "Happy place." In the verandah of one of them a woman sat weaving—just as she had when I had passed through the same spot two years before; and once more there was borne in upon me the curiously illusive nature of that which we name "time." The picture which she made as she sat in exactly the same position, going through precisely the same motions with shuttle and loom, with the same expression of detachment on her face, fitted so accurately over the impression which the same picture had left on my mind on the previous occasion, that it was difficult to realise that the two years of crowded events which had intervened, were anything more than a curtain pulled for a moment across the frame of a picture which had been all the time before me.

We had by now a tolerably extended acquaintance with Sikhim bands; and we had learned to appreciate the indigenous music of the hills. On this occasion we encountered a novel orchestra. It was a Sikhim band, certainly; but it had exchanged its instruments and, we assumed—though the point was not susceptible of proof—its melodies also, for those of Europe. It had discovered, further, that to dine to the accompaniment of music was in accordance with modern practice in the cultural centres of the West, with the result that on four consecutive evenings we dined to the accompaniment of startling and, indeed, hitherto unimagined cacophonies. When, at all too infrequent intervals, silence descended upon a bruised but grateful land it did so, to borrow an expressive phrase from Oliver Wendell Holmes, "like a poultice come to heal the wounds of sound." So far as it was possible to form a judgement, both time and manner of the various renderings laid themselves open to palpable criticism; and I momentarily expected to see the Cavalry Officer, who is appreciative of good music, wringing his hands and exclaiming in the bitterness of his distress, "O tempora! O mores!" He would have done so, I think, had his Latin run to it. As it was, he gave vent to his feelings less classically, but none the less effectively, in his own tongue. A tune bearing some distant resemblance to a Scottish air gave poignancy to the absence of the Elder. By one of those curious twists which Fate gives now and then to the orderly progress of our lives, he had been caught up for a time in the vortex of world politics and was living—I was going to say riotously, but that would, perhaps, be a misleading term—in a Paris hotel, a participant in the Peace Conference. His place was taken by one claiming acquaintance with the Lepcha tongue, whose animated dialogues with these shy denizens of the jungle, no less than his cheery companionship, contributed appreciably to the gaiety of our party.

Our first night out from Darjeeling we spent, as once before, at Namchi. From here we trekked through the lovely olive-green forest that clings to the steep sides of Tendong—the local Mount Ararat—and crossing the saddle at Damthang, "the Meadow of Mud"—muddy certainly

Plate 16.

A WOMAN OF NEPAL.

"In the verandah a woman sat weaving . . . . .

but scarcely one's idea of a meadow—dropped to the Tista river, spanned here by a frail-looking suspension bridge. The impression of frailty created by its appearance, was heightened by a notice in conspicuous lettering to the effect that no animal was to be taken across loaded—an order which truth compels me to state, was treated with haughty disdain by my muleteers, though they salved their consciences by refraining from crossing more than one at a time. A steep climb up the wooded range which here divides the waters of the Tista and Rongni rivers brought us to Song, a comfortable rest-house at 4500 feet standing under the lee of a moss-grown chorten and a picturesque mendong of weather-worn stone.

The day's journey from here to Gangtok, the modern capital of Sikhim, takes one at first through lovely forest by a path that worms its way along precipitous cliffs, to the monastery of Ramthek, an ancient institution which, we learned, had been ruled over by an unbroken succession of twenty-five lamas of the Karmapa sect. Here the lamas with the picturesque head-dress distinctive of the sect, consisting of a scarlet peak rising from an upturned brim of dark blue or black, turned out in force to welcome us. At their invitation we attended the service of the *mandala*—a daily performance in the monastery temples at which the universe and all that therein is, is offered in effigy to Buddha; and thereafter were shown the temple treasures, including some particularly fine conchs, which were blown lustily by round-faced trumpeters for our edification.

After this, a drop to the Rongni river and a climb on the far side, brought us to the capital, escorted in for the last two miles of the way by as picturesque a cavalcade as is likely to be encountered anywhere in these prosaic days —orderlies and retainers in ornately worked kilts surmounted by scarlet jerkins and flower-pot hats plumed with peacock feathers, state councillors in brightly coloured flowered Chinese silks, and—dingy and inconspicuous enough, I am afraid, in all this goodly array—ourselves in drab khaki.

We spent a pleasant day or two at Gangtok preparing for our journey up the head waters of the Tista river, and no one could have been more charming or more helpful than His Highness Tashi Namgyal, C.I.E., Maharajà of Sikhim. Quite apart from the hospitality which he showed us, he placed at our disposal the knowledge and practical assistance of his officers, amongst whom was one, Kazi Dawa Samdup, a man of learning with a good knowledge of English and a scholarly knowledge of Tibetan. His study of Tibetan manuscripts has already been responsible for results of no little interest, and since it is generally believed that many of the Sanskrit manuscripts carried into Tibet in the eighth century by Guru Padma Sambhava, from the famous university of Nalanda, are now extant only in Tibetan translations, it is probable that much valuable light may still be thrown upon the history of Mahayāna Buddhism by his researches. How far the Buddhism of High Asia has parted from the Thera Vada Buddhism of Burma and

Ceylon in fundamentals, became apparent at a very early stage in our discussions. In the Buddhism of Kazi Dawa Samdup there are most emphatically a supreme God and individual human souls. Against the famous reply of Nagasena to King Milinda, in the course of which, by taking to pieces and discarding one by one the various constituent parts of the king's chariot, such as the pole, the axle, the wheels, and so on, he showed that no such thing as a chariot, as a thing in itself, existed, and by analogy no such thing as a human soul, the learned Kazi set the remarkable contents of a Tibetan manuscript which he had recently been translating in collaboration with Mr. W. Y. Evans-Wentz, a research student of the Stanford University of California.

The manuscript is entitled the "Zab-chös-zhi-khro-gongs-pa-rang-gröl-las-bar-dohi-thös-grol-chen-mo," which may be translated as "The great liberation by hearing on the astral plane from the profound doctrine of the divine thoughts of the peaceful and wrathful deities emancipating the self." I should make it clear, perhaps, that I have relied exclusively upon Kazi Dawa Samdup, both for the transliteration of the Tibetan letters and for the meaning of the words. It is more conveniently known by its short title spelt phonetically "Pardo Todol," and freely translated by Mr. Evans-Wentz as "The Book of the Dead." The manuscript is said to be part of a series which was compiled, it is thought, under the personal direction of Guru Padma Sambhava himself. And its peculiar interest is due to the fact that it describes the experiences of the human soul between death and re-birth. And how could such a description be given if there were no such thing as a human soul? challenged the learned Kazi. How indeed?

He further drew my attention to a remarkably fine specimen of the *Si-pa-ki-khor-lo* in the royal palace, depicting on a large scale the progress of souls from world to world. In reply I pointed out that, while it undoubtedly portrayed in striking manner the various stages in the cycle of existence, it gave no indication of what was, after all, the object of Buddha's teaching, namely, the avenue of escape therefrom. He pointed to the presentation of the demon who is shown in these paintings, as holding up the wheel of life to view like a scroll, and he explained that what was displayed in the scroll was wholly within the cycle in which we were ourselves encaged, and that, for the very reason that we were ourselves within it, that which lay outside it, was beyond our power to portray.

And among other things he spoke with emotion of Spyanras-gzigs—pronounced Cheresi—the Tibetan name of the divine bodhisat Avalokita, whose image finds a place upon so many of the temple altars in Tibet and Sikhim. He is, indeed, the principal tutelary God of Tibet, the representative of Buddha and guardian of the Buddhist faith, until the expected appearance upon earth of Maitreya, the Buddha that is to come. His history is recorded in the *Mani-kah-bum*, a work attributed to King Srong-tsan-gam-po, wherein, as has already been mentioned, it is stated that he was miraculously brought into existence by Amitabha. It was on the occasion of his receiving the blessing of his spiritual creator, that he brought forth the famous prayer "Om mani padme, hum!" To enable him to discharge his duties towards Buddhism upon earth he is incarnate in each successive Dalai Lama, more usually known in Tibet, according to Colonel Waddell, under the title of Gyal-wa Rin-po-ch'e, the Great Gem of Majesty. The same authority regards this particular incarnation theory as an ingenious and calculated fiction, devised by the fifth Grand Lama and first priest-king of Tibet, Nag-wan Lo-zang, whose ambitions reached after temporal as well as spiritual power. Be that as it may, there is no doubt whatsoever of the satisfaction which the populace derives from the idea, that they possess in their ruler a God incarnate; and the esteem in which the divine Bodhisat is held, is evident to any one who has noticed the frequency with which his image is enshrined throughout the country. Indeed, we learned from Kazi Dawa Samdup, that no less than twenty-one conventional forms of it are authoritatively prescribed. And it was sufficiently clear from the whole of our discussions that, here, in its mountain home the Buddhism of the educated few as of the ignorant masses, very far from being a system of pure rationalism, is an elaborate scheme of things resting on a background of occultism, in which theurgy has completely ousted reason.

Of this one meets with constant confirmation.

One finds it, for example, in the lama dances which play so striking a part in the ceremonial of this strange religion and which, in addition to reproducing in impressive pantomime the legends of the church, aim also, by familiarising the laity with the terrifying appearance of the denizens of the unseen world, at preparing them to meet with fortitude the adventures which await them during that period, presumably, which is dealt with in the Pardo Todol. Devil-dancing seems to have been practised in Tibet before the introduction of Buddhism. The old year was expelled, and the new year ushered in, with a pantomimic display; and a form of dance also played a part in the ritual concerned with the exorcising of malignant spirits and the destruction of human enemies. The Buddhist missionaries adapted this popular adjunct of the Tibetan ritual to their own purposes, and the dances usually seen in the monasteries at the present day, represent some legend connected with the introduction and progress of the Buddhist doctrine. The one which I have seen most often is known as the Black Hat dance, and the four main scenes into which it is divided all deal with the death and subsequent fate of a Tibetan king, who became notorious as a persecutor of the Buddhist faith.

The story is a quaint one, and I tell it as it was told to me. In essence it is an illustration of the working of the doctrine of karma and re-birth; it is, therefore, a story with a moral. An element of realism is introduced by the application of the story to two actual historical figures, Ral-pa-chen, king of Tibet in the ninth century A.D., and his murderer and successor, Lang Darma, who seized the throne somewhere about the year 899 A.D. and for three years, until his own assassination, persecuted the recently established church. The prelude to the quasi-historical part of the story, that is to say, the happenings in the earlier birth which were responsible for the course which events took in the subsequent incarnation, is staged at Khatmandu, the capital of Nepal. The central figure, who, however, does not appear in the subsequent incarnation, is a certain widow, a publican grown rich on the proceeds of her trade in liquor. Assailed late in life by qualms of conscience, she seeks to atone for past misdeeds, in other words, to balance the scale in which will be weighed her accumulated merit and demerit, by the erection of a large chorten. At the ceremony of dedication, so runs the story, she was joined by her three sons. She was, however, the possessor not only of sons but of an elephant; and this sensitive beast, finding himself ignored and cast for no part in the dedicatory service, gave utterance to curses instead of prayers and vowed that in a future birth he would destroy Buddhism. Hence, as we shall see, the subsequent trouble. With this fiery and unexpected outburst on the part of an animal usually known for its intelligence and docility, that part of the story which I have called the prelude, comes to an end, and when the curtain rises again it is upon the quasi-historical episode on which the main part of the tale rests.

In due course, the eldest of the widow's three sons was re-born in Tibet, and ascended the throne under the title of King Ral-pa-chen. About the same time the elephant was born as Lang Darma, the king's younger brother. In accordance with the inexorable law of karma the king proved to be an enthusiastic patron of Buddhism, while his brother cherished sentiments of enmity towards it. At his instigation Ral-pa-chen was murdered and he himself ascended the throne, whence for three years he persecuted the church. The widow's youngest son then re-appeared upon the stage, being re-born at Lha-lung, where he entered the order under the name of Lama Pal Dorjé. And it was by his hand that the infamous Lang Darma was slain and the persecution of the church brought to an end. It is this episode which forms the subject of the Black Hat dance. I describe it as I have seen it.

From the dim recesses of the monastery building a number of mummers process into the courtyard, dressed in long flowing black robes with baggy sleeves and wearing enormous black hats. These represent the ancient devil-dancers. Disguised as one of these—so runs the story—Lama Pal Dorjé attracted the notice of Lang Darma by his dancing, and was summoned by the king to his palace. This provided the lama with the opportunity which he sought, and producing a bow and arrow from his ample sleeves he shot him. This brings to an end the first scene of the dance and, incidentally, the historical foundation of the story. Henceforth we enter realms of pure fiction.

Plate 17.

MUMMERS IN A LAMA DANCE.

"... Cemetery ghouls who perform wild gyrations round a figure sometimes of sawdust and sometimes of dough."

The next scene shows the dead king being escorted to the judgement hall of Yama, the god who is seen depicted in the wheels of life as seated on a judgement throne in the lower world, having the merit of those who are brought before him weighed in the balance against their demerit, and passing judgements and sentences in accordance with the result. The part of the escort is played by two remarkably realistic skeletons known as *Yam-duts*, or cemetery ghouls, who perform wild gyrations round a figure sometimes of sawdust and sometimes of dough, representing the dead king. The verdict of Yama is that the body is to be torn to pieces by the stag-headed dragon and scattered to the four winds of heaven.

The third scene which represents the execution of this order is a veritable *danse macabre.* The stag-headed dragon dances round gloating over his victim. He then stabs him and gores him with his horns and is joined presently by a troupe of grotesque monsters, such as might have haunted the more extravagant nightmares conjured up by the disordered imagination of the famous opium-eater, whose experiences have been so graphically depicted by the skilful pen of De Quincey. The dismemberment of the corpse proceeds to the accompaniment of a storm of unimaginable discords, given forth by a collection of instruments particularly well suited to the production of cacophonous noise; and the dance continues until the last remnants of the effigy have been scattered to the winds.

The joy of the people at the destruction of their enemy is indicated by a mendicants' dance with which the story is brought to a close. The display varies in detail, but in its main features is given in all the monasteries at which I myself have witnessed such performances. The masks and head-dresses worn are very elaborate both in colour and in design, and the dresses, especially those of embroidered Chinese silk, are often really beautiful and must be of considerable value.

On our return journey we visited the royal monastery of Fadung, a wealthy institution of great interest but somewhat difficult of access, being a toilsome journey of some hours from Gangtok; and here we witnessed a dance which I have not myself seen elsewhere. The performers, who showed great nimbleness of foot, were said to represent a type of being living only in Sang-thog Palri, the highest heaven of Guru Rimpoché. The idea seems to have been that of aerial attendants upon the fortunate dwellers in that favoured region. They are known, we were told, by the name of kh'ing.

The most interesting feature of the Fadung monastery at the present time, however, is in connection with a vacancy in its governing hierarchy. The seat of the Um-dsé or temporal head of the institution, remained empty during the service which we attended, the lead being taken by the Dorjé-lopen or spiritual head, a fine old man of eighty with a face heavily furrowed by the hand of time. The reason was explained to us. His Highness the late Maharaja of Sikhim had been the incarnation of the historic Um-dsé of Fadung; and since his death no re-incarnation had taken place. A further incarnation was expected; and a watch was being kept in the country between Fadung and Gangtok where this event was expected to take place. The re-born would be recognised, it was said, by a mark on the face.

Fadung became the royal monastery on account of its proximity to Tumlong, the ancient capital of the country, a city of which scarcely a trace now remains. Near by is another monastery of some interest, that of Labrong, one of the few institutions in Sikhim which possess a complete copy of the Teng-yur. Though small, the dimly lit temple gives an impression of subdued splendour, produced by an unusually large number of hanging banners of varying shades of gold.

CHAPTER XVI

FROM GANGTOK TO THANGU

WITH our departure from Gangtok we left behind us, for the time being, such problems as have been discussed in the preceding chapter, and devoted the whole of our attention to the marvellous scenery of the gorges through which the upper waters of the Tista force their way. Skirting round the source of the Rongni river, we dropped down to the Tista again at its confluence with a lesser stream, the Dikchu, at an altitude of little more than 2000 feet. From here we traced it faithfully to Thangu, a desolate spot of horrible memories nearly 13,000 feet up, where, to mark the end of the bridle-path, the Sikhim durbar has constructed the outermost of their bungalows in the direction of the Donkhya pass, giving elevated access—it is over 18,000 feet—to the stony highlands of Tibet. " With its wind-swept solitudes," writes one visitor, " it has a certain grim fascination : we are here upon the threshold of the snows." [1]

Before emerging on these wind-swept solitudes, however, one travels through some of the most amazing combinations of forest and mountain

[1] Mr. Percy Brown, *Tours in Sikhim.*

which it has ever been my good fortune to see. The difficulty of describing the scenery is enhanced by the lack of other examples with which to compare it. I have spent continuous months in solitary wandering over the wooded highlands of Kashmir. I have been overwhelmed in spirit by the awful desolation of the crude and empty spaces, which seem to have been thrown up into the upper air, so to speak, by some callous geological power and left forgotten, to be bleached and blistered by the sun, on the towering parapet of Western Tibet. I have bowed down in awe amidst the labyrinth of stupendous pinnacles which hedge in the listening-posts, such as Gilgit and Chilas, in the vast system of natural defences which keep silent and eternal watch over the teeming plains of Hindustan. I have likewise revelled in the exquisite scenery of the valleys of the Thian Shan — well named the Celestial mountains. And I have travelled through the tropical exuberance of Burma and Ceylon. I have also spent much time in the heart of rural Japan, and have been hauled through the giant gorges of the Yang-tsze river, giving access to those lovely uplands of Western China which go to make the provinces of Yunnan and Ssŭch'uan. But in none of these places can I recall anything quite like the crumpled forest-clad cliffs and crags, which rise precipitously on either side of the upper reaches of the Tista river.

And always as I wandered among them was I assailed with the idea, that here was no ordinary world, but the enchanted forest of my youthful dreams. We had travelled little beyond Dikchu, for example, when it became evident that somebody had been making experiments in rock gardening, experiments on a scale vast beyond the conception of any human gardener. Enormous rocks had been set up in artistic disarray upon green slopes, often on either side of the path we were following. Flowers and saxifrages clambered over them; while mosses, ferns, and creepers, more reckless or more ambitious, climbed the soaring trunks of stately trees. When the sun shone through their leafy canopy, one could almost hear the silvery tinkle of the flower bells, and when the breeze blew softly, there was much whispering among the trees. Moreover, we were entering a country reserved for Lepchas, a stumpy, flat-faced people with sallow complexions and matted black hair, just such gnomes as one would look for in the sombre depths of an enchanted forest. And their impersonation of the part was perfect when, as not infrequently happened, they emerged unexpectedly from the forest armed with bow and arrows. And as if this was not enough, the attendants thoughtfully detailed by His Highness the Maharaja to accompany us, were garbed in a manner one would look for in no one but a woodland elf.

The people themselves have strange things to tell. To us seated one day in the shade of a gaunt-looking chorten, shaggy with moss, came a village elder socially disposed. The spot was a striking one—a tongue of level land thrust out at the foot of a mountain wedge at the apex of which the waters of the Lachung and Lachen

Plate 18.

ELVES OF THE FOREST.

"The attendants detailed to accompany us were garbed in a manner one would look for in no one but a wood-land elf."

rivers mingle, to be known thenceforward as the Tista: for which reason the people have given it the name of Chung Thang, or the "marriage of the rivers." A few hundred feet above us a small gompa enshrined an image of Guru Rimpoché. Had we seen this? he asked. We had, and many other images of the great saint throughout the country-side. But there was special reason for the veneration in which he was held here. We expressed our interest in the matter, and our informant invited our attention to a mark upon a rock lying near—the imprint of the Guru's foot, it was explained. At that time, it appeared, the locality was haunted by spirits both good and evil, and in particular by a female spirit of peculiar malignity. Her the holy man shot—somewhat ungallantly as it seemed to us—in the back, and gibbeted the corpse high upon a cliff rising in our view from where we sat, from the bank of the Lachung river. The corpse being that of a spirit and not of mortal clay, did not go the way of all flesh, but remained suspended—a thing of ill-omen to the land of Sikhim. Whenever misfortune threatened the land a portion of the grizzly figure was precipitated to the valley bottom, there to vanish in fine white powder. Thus had it been immediately prior to the invasions from Nepal, later from Bhutan, and later still from British India.

Was this thing still there? we asked. Most assuredly, replied our informant. Had he himself seen it? Of course he had. Only the year before the familiar warning had been given.

He had approached the spot but had been held back by an overpowering odour. He had at once communicated news of the occurrence of the omen to the Government at Gangtok. And had any calamity ensued? we asked. It had indeed, the whole population had been decimated by a new and terrible disease to which the name of "one-stroke fever" had been given. This was unfortunately true. I had myself arranged to visit the Lachen Valley the previous autumn, but had been obliged to cancel my tour at the last moment, at the request of the Maharaja himself, owing to the havoc caused among the population by the epidemic of influenza, which swept across India like a scourge and penetrated far into the surrounding mountains. As a minor marvel, our informant pointed to a recumbent tree trunk from which a new shoot had sprung. This had lain neglected for sixty years, for the reason that it had been a talking tree, and no one dared to touch it.

As we advanced up the left bank of the river, the mountains seemed to close in upon us and the river forced its way fiercely between narrow and precipitous banks. And here the Lepchas had thrown one of their cane bridges across it, much as a monster spider might have thrown its thread. The footway consisted of a couple of bamboos, sometimes side by side, but at others one on top of the other, these being suspended by strands of fibre from two parallel ropes of twisted cane, the whole forming a V-shaped way. With every step it creaked and swayed, and since one had of necessity to look

Plate 10.

CHORTENS IN THE FOREST.

"Seated in the shade of a gaunt looking chorten, shaggy with moss . . ."

down in order to see where to place one's next step, one's gaze was being perpetually riveted on the swirling torrent, racing tumultuously thirty or forty feet below one, with the result that the swinging motion of the bridge, sufficiently unpleasant in any case, acquired an exaggerated value. Since our track still lay up the left bank of the river there was no occasion for us to cross it. We did so out of sheer bravado. And having landed on the other side, we recrossed by it out of pure necessity.

I was seated on the damp jungle-covered bank of the river replacing my foot-gear, which I had found it advisable to remove when crossing the bridge, when I discovered that the leeches had taken advantage of the situation and were fattening on my ankles. The Cavalry Officer began laughing. "What is it ?" I asked rather testily. There is nothing particularly calculated to excite laughter in the process of removing leeches from one's bleeding flesh. "Do you know what the Lepcha word for leech is ?" he asked. "No, I do not," I replied. "Joke," he said, and shouted with laughter. The Cavalry Officer, it will be seen, has a pretty sense of humour.

Before the end of the day's journey we came upon a tremendous gash in the mountain side, yawning across our course at right angles to the Tista river. Down this a volume of boiling water hurled itself under the name of the Rongrong river, sometimes racing over a rocky bed, sometimes falling sheer for hundreds of feet; and high up in mid-air, two hundred and fifty feet above the boiling cauldron at the bottom of the fall, hung suspended from cliff to cliff, two hundred and fifteen feet apart, a bridge just wide enough to admit the passage of a loaded mule. Two experiences of the kind in a single day were more than satisfying, and by the time we had crossed we felt that we had run through the whole gamut of emotions to be derived from bridges. Not far beyond this the valley of the Tista itself ran into a vast amphitheatre of wooded cliffs, from which a tangled labyrinth of immense gorges radiated, and we climbed up to Singhik, 4600 feet, where we spent the night, high up above the waters of the river.

Early morning at Singhik, provided the mist, which clings with stubborn persistence to these warm, moist valleys, is late in rising from their dank bottoms, is a revelation. On the far side of the river Nature has opened a wondrous window in the vast wall with which she has hedged it in, in the shape of the Talung valley. At the head of this valley, in the very centre of the window, so to speak, rises the soaring peak of Kanchenjunga, a marvellous picture which can scarcely be surpassed in dramatic effect in any part of the world. From one's own altitude of less than 5000 feet one's gaze is drawn across the yawning abyss of the Tista gorge, and on along the sombre vista of the Talung valley to the glistening cone, which towers skywards to a height of over 28,000 feet.

For the best part of three days we travelled through gorges comparable only with those of the Yang-tsze between Ichang and Chungking.

The volume of water pouring down the latter is greater than down the Tista, and its span is far wider. But their turbulence and narrowness give the Tista gorges a character of their own, which is accentuated by the density of the semi-tropical vegetation which clings to the precipitous mountain sides, and by the sharpness of the angle, and the towering height at which these latter prick the sky. The aggressiveness of the vegetation is amazing. Every kind of growth from minute flowers and grasses to tall timber trees struggles fiercely for foothold on the precipitous mountain slopes; and one and all emerge from the struggle triumphant, with a resulting world of riotous plant life. Mosses and lichens seize upon the surface of rocks too smooth, or too steep, to afford a resting-place for larger growths. Bamboos — and in particular a slender blue-stemmed variety with delicate feathery leaves recalling vivid impressions of the pictorial art of China and Japan—ferns, grasses, nettles, and a bewildering medley of other undergrowths wage unceasing warfare with more majestic orders. And upon the trunks and branches of these latter there flourishes a vast host of parasitic growths, from delicately tinted orchids to giant-leaved creepers.

But suddenly towards the end of the third day from Dikchu this state of things came to an abrupt end. We were following up the Lachen river, the westernmost of the two main streams which, when united, are known as the Tista, when we stepped steeply into another world. It was still a world of mountains; but their character had changed. The riotous vegetation of the sub-tropical and temperate zones had vanished and an Alpine flora bloomed in its place. We were standing on the broader bottom of an upland valley, and in an amphitheatre in the hill-side stood the little village of Lachen at a height of 8800 feet. And once more we were brought into intimate contact with India's absorbing and eternal quest.

It was brought to the fore again by our encounter with the presiding lama of the Lachen gompa, a spiritual leader of such eminence and reputation as to have earned for himself the title of Gompchen, or Great Hermit. Over a period of twenty-six years, he had been in the habit of retiring from the world from time to time and living a life of solitary meditation in a remote cave, the situation of which was pointed out to us later, high up and difficult of access, among the cliffs of an inhospitable tract of mountain above the path to Thangu. One of these periodic retirements from the world had been protracted over a period of five years, during which time he had seen no human being and had kept body and soul together on a minimum of food.

From conversation with him it appeared that he had reached the stage of Arahatship and was, therefore, beyond good and evil. We had been examining with interest a monster Mani wheel, occupying the whole of a separate temple some little distance from his own, a truly famous mechanism for the dissemination of prayer wholesale, being the largest in Sikhim, with a reputed

Plate 20.

POTHOS CREEPER CLINGING TO TREE TRUNK.

"Every kind of growth, from minute flowers and grasses to tall timber trees, struggles fiercely for foothold . . . ."

output of one and a half billion prayers per revolution; and I asked him with some curiosity how the destiny of man could be in any way influenced by such means. He admitted quite frankly that the vain repetitions, the images upon the altars, the mandalas, and all the elaborate externalism of Lamaism as ordinarily practised, meant nothing to him at all. Such things were but mummery, wholly without virtue in themselves. Their value lay in the power which they possessed of attracting the attention and occupying the mind of the ordinary man. Before parting I asked him the question which King Milinda asked the Sage Nagasena, namely, would he be re-born or would he at the close of his present life attain Nirvana? He replied that this was a very big question, the answer to which was not easy to give. That Nirvana was within his grasp was not in doubt. He was the sole arbiter of his future destiny. But it might be that at the hour of death, out of pity for the sufferings of humanity, he might decide to be born once more to extend his saving help to others.

Here we have all the conditions recorded in the Buddhist scriptures as antecedent to the final birth of Gautama as Buddha. All that was said on the subject was clearly spoken in all seriousness. Did this Tibetan priest—to all outward appearances a man differing little from the generality of mankind—believe implicitly all that he said? It is difficult to say. This, at least, is certain, the motive which impels men to leave their fellows, and for years on end, spurning the weaknesses of the flesh, to live a life of solitary confinement, must be an extraordinarily powerful one. That such lives excite admiration and respect is equally certain. The two lamas of my experience commanding the deepest and most widespread veneration are, undoubtedly, the Gompchen of Lachen and the learned principal of the Tung-kar Monastery in Chumbi, the Geshi Tromo. In each case knowledge and wisdom have been sought in solitary communing with the spirit, during long periods of confinement in remote fastnesses in the mountains cut off from the haunts of men. It was with every sign of awe and reverence that I was told how, high on the rugged sides of Cho-mo-lhari, the Geshi Tromo had sought to wrest from the great unknown something of the secret of the universe. And just as, in the case of the Gompchen, I was shown the distant site of one of his strange hermitages, so in the case of the Geshi Tromo, I had pointed out to me with pride and reverence, a speck of rock and stone just visible on a barren mountain side, as holy ground, where he had lived long periods of uninterrupted meditation.

The rigorous hardship of solitary confinement is well known. It is recognised by the Indian Penal Code, which strictly limits the term of such a sentence to one month, and further qualifies it by laying down that not more than seven days shall be so served consecutively. And it is difficult to suppose, even in these rugged and isolated corners of the world, where the standard of living is not a high one, that a man would willingly condemn himself to prolonged periods of such existence without assurance of a sustaining force beyond the experience, and perhaps even the comprehension, of the average Westerner.

* * * * * *

Beyond Lachen we took another step up and found ourselves in a typically Alpine world. The mountain sides were less completely hidden by forest, and the monotony of the eternal green of the lower valleys was broken by splashes of vivid autumn tints. Silver fir, spruce, larch, juniper, and rhododendron formed the bulk of the flora. Many of the larches had turned a rusty gold, while hips and haws shone scarlet in the sunshine and a rich variety of thorn-bushes ran through the whole scale of reds, from crimson lake to burned brick. A strange effect was produced at times by quantities of a grey-green lichen, which clung to the fir trees and streamed like great handfuls of frayed wool in the wind.

At 3.30 P.M. on the last day of October we reached the last bungalow in Sikhim, standing under a cliff in a bleak upland valley some 13,000 feet above sea-level—a lean and inhospitable land, peopled sparsely by nomad folk living in sheds roughly built of unshaped stone, and depending for their existence mainly upon herds of uncouth-looking yaks. The most conspicuous representative of the plant world was the deadly aconite, upon which one of our ponies foolishly browsed and died during the night.

A peculiarly sinister atmosphere hangs over Thangu. This was at once apparent from the tone of the remarks by travellers in the bungalow book; and before long from the feelings of *malaise* which we ourselves experienced. On one of the two nights which we spent there I was unable to sleep at all, and it was noticeable that our coolies, though hill-men themselves, suffered as much from insomnia and even more from mountain sickness than we did. The general discomfort was accentuated by the cold and the persistent mist, and in my own case by the misplaced thoughtfulness of my Indian servant, who had secretly brought with him a hot-water bottle, which he hid in my bed as a pleasant surprise on arrival at Thangu. The climate of Bengal has a perishing effect upon rubber, but it was not until I had tossed uneasily from side to side for some time that I realised that the bed-clothes were becoming inexplicably damp. Investigation brought to light the half-empty water-bottle. The Cavalry Officer never, under any circumstances, experiences any difficulty in going to sleep. He was probably the only member of the whole party that night who was enjoying unruffled repose. But the joke was too good to be enjoyed by myself, and a solid half-hour was cut out of his night while I explained it to him and then looked on while he put matters right.

* * * * * *

Thangu, like Lingtu, has witnessed the making of history. The Anglo-Chinese convention of 1890, which was an outcome of the happenings at Lingtu, defined the boundary between Sikhim and Tibet as the crest of the mountain range separating the waters flowing into the Sikhim Tista and its affluents from the waters flowing into the Tibetan Mochu and northwards into other rivers in Tibet. "The line," it was stated, "commences at Mount Gyi-mo-chi on the Bhutan frontier and follows the above-mentioned water-parting to the point where it meets Nepal territory." The Tibetans, however, as has already been remarked, studiously ignored the convention. They did more. They uprooted the boundary pillars erected with painstaking care by Mr. White, the British Resident in Sikhim, and, in this neighbourhood, established an outpost at a spot which some enterprising map-maker has named Giagong. Now Giagong is a spot on a stream which indisputably flows into the Sikhim Tista. It is west of the Donkhya La, which is a pass over the crest of the mountain range referred to in the convention, and it is south of the Kangra La, another pass over the same range; and by no possible argument, consequently, could it be made out to be on the Tibetan side of the frontier laid down by the convention.

The Tibetans had retired from Giagong temporarily in 1902 as a result of the personal intervention of Mr. White. But with his departure from the spot, they had returned. And in July 1903 the remote bungalow of Thangu extended its shelter to three men who were destined to play a part of paramount importance in moulding the future of the peoples of the Eastern Himalayas. These men were Colonel (now Sir F.) Younghusband, Mr. Claud White, and Captain (now Colonel) O'Connor, the first the leader and the last the interpreter of the subsequent mission to Lhasa.

In due course the party proceeded to Khamba Jong, the nearest fort on the Tibetan side of the frontier. The Chinese, however, to quote Colonel Younghusband's own words, "showed indifference and incompetence and the Tibetans pure obstruction,"[1] and three months passed with no progress even towards the opening of negotiations, to show. The Tibetans devoted the whole of their energies to abortive attempts at persuading the British envoys to return to Giagong, or failing that, to Yatung. Their attitude was exemplified by the proceedings of the most friendly of them all, the ingenuous abbot of Shigatse, who came down from the famous monastery of Tashi-lhumpo to explain to Colonel Younghusband the embarrassment which was being caused to his superior, the Tashi Lama, by the presence of the British at Khamba Jong. He was, according to Colonel Younghusband, "a charming old gentleman." But "whatever intellectual capacity he may have had was not very apparent to the casual observer, and he corrected me when I inadvertently let slip some observation implying that the earth was round, and assured me that when I had lived longer in Tibet, and had time to study, I should find that it was not round but flat, and not circular but triangular; like the bone of a shoulder of mutton."[2] After this one feels that a reasonable measure of scepticism was permissible, even when the good abbot issued a solemn warning that he had made a divination that Yatung was the

[1] *India and Tibet*, by Sir F. Younghusband, K.C.S.I., K.C.I.E.

[2] *Ibid.*

place where negotiations would be carried on quickest.

In the end the baffling inertia of the Tibetans proved too much for the patient perseverance of the British, and Colonel Younghusband retired, not to Giagong or Yatung, but to Simla, there to arrange for the expedition which was so soon to embark upon its historic enterprise.

The farce played for three months at Khamba Jong, if not without its humour for those who took part in it, was also not without its lesson for the British Government at home. It gave point to what the Government of India had already urged, namely, that the suzerainty of China over Tibet was "a constitutional fiction —a political affectation" which had only been maintained on account of its convenience to both parties. China was willing, nay, anxious to adopt an enlightened policy, but her desire was always defeated by the "short-sighted stupidity of the lamas." Tibet on her part desired nothing more than to join hands with us in throwing open her country to trade, but was prevented from doing so by "the despotic veto of the suzerain."

The summing-up of the situation in the same despatch, the vigorous language of which left no doubt as to its authorship, was sufficiently emphatic—"this solemn farce has been re-enacted with a frequency that seems never to deprive it of its attractions or its power to impose."[1] And, as we have seen, it was re-enacted once more

[1] Despatch from the Government of India to the Secretary of State, 1899, quite clearly drafted by Lord Curzon himself.

at Khamba Jong before its run was at length brought to a close.

* * * * * *

During our day's halt at Thangu we climbed the steep spur behind the bungalow, an offshoot of the range which culminates in the gigantic peak of Kanchenjhau, 22,700 feet; and on reaching a summit at about 16,000 feet we decided to wait patiently for the clouds to lift. This they did somewhat unexpectedly at mid-day, disclosing a stupendous panorama, in which Kanchenjhau and Chomiomo, 22,430 feet, were prominent features. Far below us the streams of the Lachen and its tributaries shone like silver threads in the sombre depths of a vast abyss. And then, before we had had time to drink in the whole majestic grandeur of that which lay around us, Nature stretched forth a clammy hand and once more drew an impenetrable curtain across our vision. It is at her whim and not at man's demand that she discloses the glories of her handiwork; and she is, alas, of a wayward disposition.

CHAPTER XVII

THE WAY TO THE ETERNAL SNOWS

If from the terrace of Government House, Darjeeling, one looks in a direction thirteen degrees west of north, one can see clearly with the naked eye on a fine day, a small black point impinging upon the hem of the snow-white garment in which the great group of peaks which cluster round Kanchenjunga is ever dressed. Investigation goes to show that this small black object is a conical peak of augen-gneiss, 15,810 feet above sea-level, raised up like a tower of observation on the glacis of the eternal snows. Its distance from Darjeeling is thirty-five miles. But that is as the crow flies; for a biped it is an entirely different story. For between the spur on which stands Darjeeling, and Kabur—the name given on the maps to the peak in question —there has been fashioned by the giant hand of Nature a series of deep, heavily-wooded valleys which stretch in parallel lines like well-constructed systems of defence works, athwart the line of his advance. And across these he has perforce to make his way, before he may stand even upon the threshold of the great white heart of the Himalayan world.

The autumn of the year 1920 was a memorable one in the eastern Himalayas. The monsoon had withdrawn earlier than usual, and even dripping Darjeeling was short of its normal rainfall by nearly twenty inches. And as we set forth upon our enterprise, the bright October sun searched to their depths the cavernous forests into which we were about to make our way. During a long morning we dropped down through five thousand feet of tea, passing through famous gardens whose products find their way into the households of five continents; and in due course reached the little mart of Singla Bazar. We had accomplished the descent of the first line of defence, and before nightfall had climbed up the steep slope on the far side, passing near the summit through masses of sweet-smelling jasmin, and had trekked along a cultivated shoulder past an inevitable gompa, to the bungalow of Chakung —a journey of about eighteen miles in all.

The following day we were involved in two such descents and ascents before we reached the pass where the bridle-paths from Darjeeling, Pemiongchi, and Dentam meet; and then after two miles of comparatively level going through shady forest reached Rinchenpong—thirteen and a half miles in all. From Rinchenpong we dropped five miles steeply to the Kulhait river, and then climbed about six miles to Pemiongchi. Two miles short of the latter place stands Geysing, a small hamlet famous for its mendong or mani wall, a thick wall-like structure as broad as it is high, and in this case two hundred yards long, faced with stone slabs on which is carved the mystic prayer, "Om mani padme, hum!" and supported at each end by chortens. The characters were beautifully carved on some of the stones, and one bore an inscription stating that the building was erected by the third incarnation of Lhatsen Chembo "to the glory of the king and the good of the country" some three hundred years ago. We were to hear a good deal more of Lhatsen Chembo in the course of the next few days.

In the meanwhile it may be explained that the construction of a mendong is one of the various alternative methods of acquiring merit, which are open to the devout followers of Lamaism. From the point of view of the general public it possesses certain advantages over some of the other methods which have been described, since a share in the accumulating merit may be acquired by the addition of a carved slab, by any one who cares to go to the comparatively small trouble and expense of arranging for such an addition. These buildings invariably run down the centre of the road, so that they may be left on the right of the passer-by from whichever direction he is approaching; and some merit apparently accrues from thus passing them. At any rate, on arrival at the mendong of Geysing, my attention was attracted by a familiar figure—that of an aged man in ragged garments walking slowly backwards and forwards the length of the mendong, fingering his beads, and turning a prayer-wheel the while. The scene was familiar because I had seen it all when I happened to be journeying through the same spot six months before. What I saw now was identical in every detail with what I had seen then. The same figure in the same tattered clothes walked with the same measured tread, the same two hundred paces backwards and forwards on either side of the mendong. With the same regularity he told his beads and twirled his prayer-wheel; and with the same mechanical lack of understanding he mumbled the same musty incantations.

He provided a striking example of one of the main pillars upon which the practice of Lamaism rests—reverence for repetition and an unquestioning faith in number. One meets with it on all sides and in an amazing variety of forms. On the walls of the temple at Pemiongchi there are paintings of the image of Buddha repeated a thousand times. Cheresi, the patron god of Tibet, is represented sometimes with four hands, sometimes with eleven heads, and sometimes with a thousand—used conventionally to signify large numbers—eyes. In a chamber in the body of the great golden image of Buddha Maitreya which had recently been set up in the monastery at Ghum—an image so large that it sits with the lower half of its body on the ground floor while the head and shoulders penetrate the ceiling and appear upon the upper story—I was told there were one thousand six hundred small images, replicas possibly of the image in whose bosom they rested.

In an earlier chapter I have made mention of a vast abyss spanned by a slender suspension bridge on the track up the Tista valley, between Dikchu and Singhik. It is called the gorge of the Rong-rong Chu. The meaning of the word *Rong* is "deep gorge," and here, too, we find that local feeling has been able to give adequate expression to its sense of the magnitude of the chasm, only by having recourse to repetition. That the essence of the method of intercession, of which the ubiquitous prayer-flag and mani-wheel are the instruments, is repetition, must have been made abundantly clear by what has already been written. Throughout the country a perfectly astonishing output of energy is daily being devoted to getting things repeated. If in the vocabulary of the country any place were found for the word "monotonous," for the vast majority of the people it would certainly possess no meaning.

At Pemiongchi we were on the crest of the last of the series of ridges stretching across the line of our advance. On the far side of the valley across which we gazed from the bungalow verandah, rose the stupendous mass of the Kanchenjunga group. And here a re-ordering of our caravan became necessary. We were leaving bridle-paths and rest-houses behind us. The hill pony was no longer a practical proposition, and though for one march more we had the assistance of some local steeds that performed amazing feats of mountain-climbing with the agility and assurance of goats, we had thereafter to rely upon our own powers.

Our objective for the first day out from Pemiongchi was a cultivated plateau on the far side of the valley of the Rathong, and so steep were the sides of the valley that the scattered farmsteads of Yuk-sam appeared to be little more than a stone's-throw from the bungalow verandah. The march thither, however, is not so simple as one would suppose. One cannot drop straight down to the Rathong river and climb straight up the other side, for there is neither track nor bridge and one has to make a detour first down to a tributary of the Rathong, named the Rungbi, and then up a spur dividing it from yet another stream. This spur we crossed below the Malli gompa, marched for a mile along its northern slope and then dropped to the second tributary. A farther climb followed to the summit of the ridge dividing this tributary from the main stream, and here we were welcomed by the inhabitants of a few scattered houses which have come to be regarded as a village, upon which some one has conferred the name of Tingling. So far as we could judge, in point of actual distance we were still as far from Yuk-sam as we had been at Pemiongchi, and the valley of the Rathong was still to cross. Cheered by the marwa with which we were regaled by the good folk of Tingling, we resumed the road with renewed vigour and made short work of the two miles' descent which brought us at last to the banks of the Rathong river. The climb on the far side was extremely severe; but it was wonderfully picturesque, taking us, towards the finish, through a thicket of closely growing, slender-stemmed bamboos among which bloomed some lovely bushes of Luculia, ablaze with great clusters of pink flowers.

At Yuk-sam, "the place of the three lamas,"

Plate 21.

ON THE ROAD TO THE ETERNAL SNOWS.

"A re-ordering of our caravan became necessary, the hill pony was no longer a practical proposition."

our tents were pitched on a slight eminence overlooking scattered farmsteads, consisting of substantial buildings of unshaped stone and timber worn grey by the weather. It possesses a peculiar interest, for it is here that the history of Sikhim as a civilised state may be said to have begun, and we halted a day to examine the traces which still exist to give support to the story of these important happenings, which is current at the present day.

Among these is the monastery of Dubdi, perched on a wooded cone some hundreds of feet above the plateau. On the way to it we passed two very fine specimens of large and brilliantly painted prayer-cylinders, fitted with water-wheels which were kept in continuous motion by a mountain stream—witnesses to an ingenuity almost equal to his reverence for repetition, on the part of their fortunate owner. The monastery is situated on a terrace from which is obtained a commanding view over the surrounding country. Fine specimens of the juniper tree, the seeds of which are said to have been brought from Tibet some three centuries ago, form conspicuous objects in the monastery enclosure. In the building itself are images and paintings such as may be seen in many other similar buildings. The image of Guru Rimpoché occupies the place of honour over the centre of the altar; but not far away is an image painted green which we were told was that of Lhatsen Chembo. Other images there were—male and female—of a character suggestive of the eroticism which had done so much to discredit Buddhism in its later phases in the land of its origin. And among the mural decorations I noticed a pictorial "Wheel of life" and also representations of the kh'ing flying in the azure heights of Sang-thog Palri, which we had seen so realistically depicted in the display of dancing given to us at the royal monastery of Fadung.

But the main interest of the Dubdi monastery is centred in its history. It is claimed for it that it was the first monastery built in Sikhim; and if one cares to do so, one may listen to the tale of the founding of the state and have pointed out to one from the terrace as it proceeds, the monuments which mark the sites of the main episodes in a dramatic story. The hero is Lhatsen Chembo—here one is referred to the green image in the temple building—a Buddhist saint who travelled from Tibet and, making his way over the wild and inhospitable passes from the north, came somewhere about the middle of the seventeenth century to Yuk-sam. Here he was met by two other lamas, one of whom had travelled from the south and the other from the west—hence, you are reminded, the name of the place signifying "the three lamas."

The country was a wild one, peopled by primitive and ignorant Lepchas, and after consultation it was decided that if religion was to flourish, a king and a stable form of government must be set up. Acting in accordance with an ancient prophecy, messengers were sent towards the east to search for a man of the name of Pun-tsok. In due course the man was found and conducted to the three lamas at Yuk-sam, who anointed him with holy water and crowned him king of Sikhim. Here one's attention is directed to a huge stone chorten marking the spot where the coronation took place. Later in the day we visited this interesting spot and found beside the chorten, a rough stone seat and a small shrine. The former was said to be the throne on which the newly appointed king was crowned. In the latter were four images representing Lhatsen Chembo and his two companions, one a lama of the Kardokpa and the other of the Nadakpa sect, and Pun-tsok.

According to the lamas of Dubdi, their monastery is the only building dating from the days of Lhatsen Chembo which survives. But they point out the sites of three other buildings which have passed away. A clump of four tall junipers marks the site of a monastery established by the lama of the Kardokpa sect; a rocky mound and two juniper trees on the edge of the ground on which we ourselves were camped, that of a monastery founded by his companion of the Nadakpa sect; and on an eminence by itself a chorten now stands where stood the house occupied by the newly crowned king. So much for history.

The clouds which had been gathering ever since we had left Pemiongchi at last came down in rain, and the night of October the 25th was a wet one. Yuk-sam was the uttermost outpost of comparative civilisation on the line of our advance, and a walk of twenty minutes on the morning of the 26th served to put it behind us. After this we entered a land where Nature reigned supreme. A narrow track, varying from eighteen inches to two feet in breadth, switch-backed along a steep mountain side high above the left bank of a turbulent torrent, the Praig-chu. The vegetation was so thick that it was difficult to see more than a few yards in any direction, and a small open spot a few miles from Yuk-sam, from which a glimpse of that place could be caught, was accorded a wholly spurious importance.

At 10 A.M. the rain became heavy, and at the end of the five or six miles we camped, pitching our tents here and there wherever a piece of ground sufficiently level for the purpose could be found. The spot was known locally as Nibi-tha, meaning "the pair of rocks"—though rocks there were in unlimited number. What it lacked in convenience, viewed from the stand-point of a camping-ground, it made up in other respects, for it was wildly picturesque. We were, however, scarcely in a mood to exalt the picturesque, for two matters of much more immediate importance thrust themselves into the forefront of all our cogitations. These were the weather—a banal and well-worn topic certainly, but one of more than ordinary importance on the present occasion, and the character of the route which lay immediately before us.

We had some grounds for apprehension in an account of both left by a writer who had travelled over the same ground some years before.[1] Of Jongri and Kabur, our first objectives above the forest zone, he had written: "We reached

[1] Mr. W. H. Buchan. See *Blackwood's Magazine* for April 1912.

Jongri in mist, in mist we made an assault on the rock peak of Kabur, in mist we left." His account of the country which had to be traversed before the immense zone of forest was finally left behind, was even more depressing. Mr. Buchan wrote of it in reverse so to speak; that is to say, his account was of the descent from Jongri to Yuk-sam, and it acquired, consequently, added poignancy as we brooded over it, from the knowledge ever present to our minds, that the 7000 feet of descent which he so vividly described was in our case to be 7000 feet of violent ascent. First we learned there was "a mud slide of 6000 feet ending in a giant tropical forest and a wet leech-bitten camp at the junction of the Praig-chu and the Rathong." Mr. Buchan then went on to state quite definitely that the country between that point and Yuk-sam was one which he had no desire to see again. He explained that he had sent out a man a month before to examine the track and that he had returned to report it impossible for any sahib. His own comment upon the report was terse and significant—"he exaggerated only a little," he wrote. And this, his considered opinion, was based on his own experience, which was conveyed to us in the following graphic words: "My recollection is of sharp rocks, fallen trees, black mud and treacherous forest mould, steep rock staircases streaming with water, logs laid along the edge of space, ankle-twisting descents and unnecessary climbs, steamy airless heat, unending ridges of thick oppressive forest, clearings that promised the end and always disclosed another deep bend and another ridge. The path was overgrown with thick vegetation. Vicious great nettles stung the hands, leeches dropped on the head and neck and joined forces with invaders from below until the last vestige of temper went and human nature was laid bare to its elements." With the ground oozing moisture under our feet, with the rain beating down on the sodden flies of our tents, and with great waves of clammy mist winding themselves round the dripping trees, we had ample grounds for the pessimism to which the account gave rise.

This pessimism, fortunately, was not justified by subsequent experience. We had chosen our season better than Mr. Buchan, who had started forth on his adventure in September. Moreover, we were fortunate in that the year was marked by an early withdrawal of the monsoon. And we were much indebted to His Highness the Maharaja for his thoughtfulness in ordering the clearing and, where possible, the improvement of the track. These various circumstances combined to defeat to a great extent the expected onslaught of leeches, tree-ticks, and stinging plants, and to ease our passage of the great ascent.

For four miles beyond Nibi-tha the track switchbacked through soaking vegetation and then lurched down to the waters of the Praig-chu, which it crossed at an altitude of about 7000 feet. A steep and laborious climb of 3000 feet on the far side satisfied us for the day, and we camped in a clearing surrounded by clumps of bamboos thriving in a forest of tall timber trees. The character of the vegetation was in itself sufficient to inform us that we had reached the upper stratum of the forest zone. During the earlier part of the day our path had been strewn with the acorns of different varieties of mountain oak. By the time we halted both silver fir and rhododendron had put in a welcome appearance. Most welcome of all was a signal change in the atmospheric conditions. When we sat down to our evening meal at 6.30 P.M. we were wrapped in dense mist. But unseen forces were at work. A north wind was shepherding the clouds down from the heights above, and he proved a faithful shepherd, for an hour later they had all passed us by, and a silver moon, one day past the full, shone down upon us from a cloudless sky. Far down in the lower valleys we could see the clouds stacked in great piles for the night. The coming of the north wind exerted a beneficial influence upon the remainder of our trip. It gave us clear weather during the whole of our sojourn among the eternal snows.

The following morning we climbed steadily up the face of what subsequent examination proved to be a huge forest-clad wedge, piled up in the apex of an angle formed by the junction of the Rathong and Praig-chu. The change in the character of the vegetation became more pronounced as the morning wore on. Oaks, maples, and other umbrageous trees completely disappeared. Rhododendrons increased in quantity but decreased in size. Silver firs became numerous, and openings amongst the trees showed that at last the forest was thinning out. On one occasion we obtained a wonderful picture of the world that lay ahead of us. Through a frame of fir trees rose the snow-white cone of Pandim, pure and inaccessible like the heart of—a child. A little to the right was Jubonu, rising from a long line of serrated black rock flecked with snow where snow could find a foothold, which ran down till it became lost among the wooded spurs below.

In the hope of emerging from the forest before the mid-day clouds came down, we pushed rapidly on; but it was not until we had been climbing steeply for four hours that we left the last of the rhododendrons—other than the dwarf variety which accompanied us right up to the moraines and glaciers themselves—behind us, and found ourselves on the edge of a vast bare and stony slope, which spread itself in crumpled folds below the black cone of augen-gneiss which had first attracted our gaze from Darjeeling. For us the summit of the first small eminence above the forest zone was the meeting-place of two widely different worlds. Behind us was a land of suffocating forest: in front vast open spaces with soaring peaks cutting sharply into the surrounding vault of blue. For our coolies, too, it apparently marked the meeting of two different worlds. Behind was the world of tree sprites and woodland elves: in front a world guarded by other, and, I think, more formidable divinities. The crossing of this border-land was not effected without due ceremony. Prayer-flags were attached to a cairn of stones and the guardian spirits of the mountains were addressed in tones that sounded almost ribald. At least I was puzzled to decide whether the lusty outpourings to which I listened could be the utterance of an invocation or the defiant hurling of a challenge.

Not far beyond the last of the thickets of rhododendrons stands a rough shed of stone, the home of two yak-herds who tend their charges in these high places during the summer months, a fact which entitles the spot to a definite location on the map under the name of Jongri. We had reached the threshold of the snows.

CHAPTER XVIII

AMID THE ETERNAL SNOWS

WITH twilight came frost, and with the frost that hushed stillness which so often accompanies very low temperatures. Overhead a brilliant moon swung serenely across a velvet sky. The stillness was enhanced, rather than disturbed, by a haunting chant that rose from the shelter of a rock a little distance from our tents—and reminded us that we were accompanied by the provost-marshal of the Pemiongchi monastery, a man to whom the secret places of these vast solitudes were as an unsealed book.

Every year in the seventh month a delegation of lamas from Pemiongchi—sometimes as many as eight in number, but in any case not less than four—toils up the steep ascent which now lay behind us, crosses the Gochak La, the "lock pass"—incorrectly given on the maps and in all the books which I have come across as Guicha La—and proceeds to a cave hidden away in the moraine on the far side, and there performs such rites and ceremonies as are ordained for the propitiation of the great spirit incarnated in this vast abode of snow. The Gochak La is consequently well known to the lamas, and as a matter of fact is specifically mentioned in the *Ten-pa Ge-che*, a volume compiled under the instructions of Lhatsen Chembo, a copy of which exists in the library of the Pemiongchi monastery.

It was this famous pass that was the Mecca of our present pilgrimage; but before a start could be made various precautionary measures were deemed necessary by our followers to ward off adverse influences. The lama from Pemiongchi threaded his way through the mazes of an elaborate ritual, in the course of which he made propitiatory offerings at a rough stone altar erected at one end of a crude stone temple, standing upon a ridge above our camp. The Lepchas with us, a people who I believe call themselves Rong-pa, meaning "people of the valleys," but who were blasphemously called Mong-pa, meaning "monkey people," by others among our followers, indulged in more sanguinary rites involving the sacrifice of a yak. The head and skin of the slaughtered animal were carried with due solemnity to the summit of the ridge and there offered to what fantastic creation of Lepcha imagination I know not. Fortunately this spirit required not the carcase, so that, almost by a dispensation of Providence, as it seemed, there was much good meat for his devout worshippers. The Cavalry Officer, who on my behalf had settled the account for the yak with its owner, ruminating upon these rites and their aftermath, guessed that the Lepchas were not quite so simple a folk as was generally supposed.

Not far from the rude stone temple are a number of chortens, and in particular a group of four, attaching to which is a history of some interest. There is preserved in Tibet a book entitled *Gurui Lungten*, or "The Book of the Prophecies of the Guru," and therein it is written that, following upon strife between Cheresi and one of his disciples, the former would be driven from Tibet. Now Cheresi, as has already been explained, is incarnate upon earth in the body of the Dalai Lama. I have also recorded, in describing our visit to the Chumbi valley, how in the year 1910 the Dalai Lama fled from his capital pursued by a body of Chinese. The day of the fulfilment of at least one of the prophecies of the Guru had clearly dawned, for was not the Chinese Emperor a disciple of the supreme pontiff of the Buddhist church? Fortunately the Guru, with a foresight and consideration which cannot be too greatly admired, left elaborate instructions as to the procedure to be followed when these dire happenings should come to pass; and in the seclusion of his retreat at Darjeeling the Dalai Lama took counsel with his wise men as to the steps to be taken to carry out the injunctions of the sacred text.

The upshot of these mysterious conclaves was the preparation of seven vessels of copper destined to convey to certain designated places, consecrated treasure. The actual contents are said to have been rice and other grain, diamonds, emeralds and other precious stones, gold and silver, and in the centre of these, rolled up in the form of small columns, beautifully inscribed manuscripts of sacred texts. After many days, during which the process of consecrating these offerings proceeded in the temporary abode of the Dalai Lama, they were despatched to their several destinations. A party under the personal direction of the Abbot of the Sera-dubdi monastery, which lies between Shigatse and Gyangtse in Tibet, proceeded to Jongri and there constructed the four chortens in which four of the sacred vessels were immured. A fifth is said to have been placed in the cave beyond the Gochak La, and the remaining two in secret places among the cliffs rising to the north of the Talung glacier. The efficacy of these measures is not open to question, for have not the Chinese vanished from the face of Tibet, and does not the Dalai Lama sit once more in the seats of the mighty high up behind the massive walls of the Potala, the ark of the holy city of Lhasa ?

From our camp at Jongri the view to the north and east was cut off by the ridge in question; but once the summit of this was reached, the eastern half of the mass of snow peaks which clusters round Kanchenjunga burst upon our gaze in all its splendour. Huge bastions of naked rock filled in the foreground of the picture upon which we gazed, and above and beyond these towered the Pandim-Jubonu group. In front of us a great gulf opened in the earth's surface—the upper valley of the Praig-chu, down to whose waters we zigzagged steeply, a drop of about 1500 feet. It is a lovely valley hedged in with cliffs and peaks, the torrent's banks clothed with rhododendrons and silver firs and great splashes of scrub resembling heath, russet and crimson in the bright rays of the sun. Crossing the river we proceeded up the left bank and camped above the tree-line at an altitude of 13,000 feet. Here, as at Jongri, the rough shelter of a yak-herd entitles the spot to a name upon the map. The name by which it is known to the few travellers who have penetrated to it, as also to the compilers of maps, is Aluk-thang. None of those with us, however, recognised such a name, and to lamas, coolies, and yak-herds alike the place was Wangla-thang, so called on account of a root, the *wangla*—a curious small growth like a baby's hand with its five fingers—which was shown to us and which was credited with medicinal properties.

The head of the valley up which we were marching is choked with the moraines of two mighty systems of glaciers, those of Pandim and Kabru, whose meeting has produced a horrifying chaos of stone and rubble. Up this we climbed and, passing a small tarn under a beetling black cliff, came some little farther distance on to two sandy flats, the dry beds of perished lakes. These are known as Chema-thang, the sandy place. Pushing on past these we came to a small circular grass-grown flat at the upper extremity of the valley, hedged in by the stupendous cliffs of the Kanchenjunga and Kabru groups on one side and of Pandim on the other. A vast glacier came down to the rim of this basin, in which we pitched our tents for the night, with the Gochak La east-north-east and straight above us. The altitude registered by the aneroid was 15,600 feet and during the night we were treated to twenty-four

Plate 22.

PANDIM, 22,100 FEET.

"In front of us a huge gulf opened into the earth's surface—the upper valley of the Praigchu."

degrees of frost, reducing everything liquid in our tents to a state of solidity.

East of camp the lovely cone of Pandim rose gloriously to a height of 22,000 feet, and from behind its massive silhouette the sun rose on November the 1st in a cloudless sky. The climb up the pass was a stiff one, at first over boulders and rubble, and then up a steep snow-slide in which we cut steps as we went. The pass is a nick in an off-shoot from Pandim, and with our backs to the latter mountain we were faced with a vast circular sweep of mountains forming a bizarre world of snow and ice. On our left were the mighty abutments of Kabru, 24,000 feet; facing us was Kanchenjunga, 28,146 feet; on our right front Simvu, 22,300 feet; while between us and the latter peak gaped the huge gulf of the Talung valley, winding its way crookedly round vast outlying spurs of Pandim.

It is easy to understand that such works of Nature impel man to worship. Vast, silent, immovable, they stand for permanence in a world of flux. To the animist they are the embodiment of inexorable power, to the pantheist the incarnation of the sublime. Before we left the pass we were to see them undergo a dramatic transfiguration. From a glorious incarnation of the sublime they became a fierce embodiment of wrath. For up the draughty channel of the Talung valley angry clouds came eddying, transforming the expression of serene repose on the face of the great white world to an angry scowl. It was symbolical of the storm of anger and hatred which, far away in the plains of India,

N

over the frost-bound stretches of Russia—yea, and amid the green fields and beneath the soft breezes of the Emerald Isle—was sweeping over the world of man.

The ascent to the summit of the pass, 16,400 feet, had taken us two hours; I accomplished the descent in forty minutes. From the site of our night's camp we marched back across the stony abomination of desolation where the moraines meet; along the broad bottom of the upper Praig-chu valley, brown now except for patches of scrub juniper, but in the summer, according to our guides, a sea of green grass and flowers; past a series of mendongs—strange example of misplaced piety—until we came to our tents pitched once more at Wangla-thang.

The afternoon of November the 2nd saw us back at Jongri, and on the 3rd a short but extraordinarily beautiful march brought us to the banks of a mountain torrent, the Churong Chu. The meaning of the name is "the waters of the narrow gorge," and no more apt selection could have been made. Down a steep wall hemming in the valley our path zigzagged, now running under the lee of a huge cliff of black rock, now plunging precipitously into dense thickets of rhododendrons. Opposite to our camp, pitched on the left bank of the torrent, a huge volume of water came foaming down the mountain side, and the noise of it in the silence of the night, as it raced to join the waters of the Churong Chu, was like the oncoming surge of a mighty ocean breaking itself upon some vast rock-girt shore. The depth of the valley between its

Plate 23.

KANCHENJUNGA, 28,146 FT. FROM THE GOCHAK LA, 16,400 FT.

"A vast circular sweep of mountains forming a bizarre world of ice and snow."

enclosing walls became apparent when the sun, on a cloudless day, left our camp at 2.15 P.M., and the shadow which spread over the valley gradually climbed up its eastern wall, the top of which it did not reach until 4.30 P.M. At the head of the valley a soaring snow-clad peak glowed pink in the sunset until 5 P.M., when it rapidly took on the cold, grey garment of night.

From the valley of the Churong Chu the day's march began with an ascent of nearly 2000 feet to a bare saddle, whence on looking back we obtained an impressive view. Among the snow-peaks which could be picked out in the panorama were Kang, standing like a sentinel over the pass of the same name on the west, Little Kabru, Kabru, the Dome and the Forked Peak in the centre, and Pandim, Jubonu, and Narsing — more correctly Gnarseng, "the upturned nose" — on the east. From here we crossed a huge corrie, and then had a long march switchbacking along the steep northern wall of the Rathong valley. Finally we nose-dived down an almost perpendicular descent to the river itself and, crossing it, camped in a pretty clearing in a forest of rhododendron and silver fir, with rocky peaks rising on all sides of us. The clearing is known locally as Gamo-thang.

Once more the day started with a stiff climb, this time of 2400 feet to the O-ma La—the Milk Pass—14,650 feet. The view from here was stupendous. Looking back over the valley from which we had climbed we were confronted with an arc of snow little short of 180 degrees, beginning with the Everest group on the left, taking in the Kabru group in the centre, and continuing through Kanchenjunga to Pandim, Jubonu, and Gnarseng. Away to the right of these the snow-clad ranges of the Tibetan borderland were limned in against a turquoise sky, conspicuous among them, rising to 22,700 feet, the huge pile of Kanchenjhau. Farther east still the Nathu and Jelap passes which we had crossed two years before, were clearly marked, and beyond them again a rugged chain of mountains merging imperceptibly into the distant highlands of Bhutan. The other half of the circle viewed from the same spot presented an exquisite picture of wooded hills and valleys dissolving gradually in the far-off plains. The ground on which we stood was rocky and bare but for a carpet of dwarf shrubs and withered grasses, with here and there the gaunt stalks of giant rhubarb standing from three to four feet in height. In the summer there must be a wonderful wealth of herbage: now all was brown, seared by the autumn frosts. The scene was wintry. The iron had entered into the ground, and on all sides huge icicles hung from the rocks like monster stalactites.

From the O-ma La we journeyed across bare wind-swept uplands until the great snowy ranges of Nepal came into sight, and on November the 5th crossed a succession of rugged passes, the Dui La or Devil's Pass, 14,900 feet, the Tag La or Tiger Pass, and the Ghara La, 14,000 feet, which took us across the frontier, and, marching high up, along the eastern wall of the lovely valley of the Yangwa, camped on a small saddle known locally as Migo-thang. From here we travelled along the watershed which forms the boundary between Nepal and Sikhim. Instead of switchbacking along some precipitous mountain side as we had so often done of late, we did so along a veritable razor's edge, often, literally, not more than four or five feet in breadth. A fall on one side would have landed one hundreds of feet below in the dark-green depths of the wooded valleys of Sikhim, on the other in those of Nepal.

Our last camp was in a small fold of the ground on the frontier near a spot called Naya. From here a tramp of five or six miles, still along the boundary, brought us to Chiabanjan on the bridle-path between Phalut and Dentam. Here we were on familiar ground; ponies were awaiting us and we travelled leisurely along the well-known track to Ghum. The forest possessed its never-ending fascination, and we noted with interest the change which takes place in its appearance between spring and autumn. The rhododendron is no longer in flower, and of the Alpine flowers the purple aconite—one of four varieties—seemed to be the only one in bloom. In the neighbourhood of Tonglu, at 10,000 feet, the dark green of the forest was picked out with patches of shimmering silver, the foliage of the *Pyrus lanata*, and conspicuous among other forest trees was an Araliaceae, the *Heptapleurum impressum*, which caught one's eye with its dark-green hanging leaves.

On November the 10th we were entertained by a party of mummers, brought up from a neighbouring hamlet by the village head-man, in celebration of the Dewali or "Feast of Lamps," a festival observed on the day of the new moon in the month of Kartikka (October-November). The celebration lacked the picturesqueness which characterises its observance in the plains, where, during the short Eastern twilight, parties of girls and young women steal silently down to the river ghats bearing with them little earthen lamps. These they set afloat with eager hearts, praying for them a safe journey. For if the light goes out, misfortune awaits the owner; but if the tiny vessel is carried away on the bosom of the waters with its slender wick aflame, the year will bring with it happiness and good fortune.

But it served to apprise us that we had reached the haunts of man; and, indeed, but three days later we found ourselves caught up once more on the swiftly-flowing stream of life in Calcutta.

CHAPTER XIX

A JOURNEY TO PHARI

DURING the summer of 1921 I carried on a fitful correspondence with His Highness Sir Uggyen Wang-chuk, G.C.I.E., K.C.S.I., Maharaja of Bhutan. Such correspondence could not, in fact, be other than intermittent. In the first place His Highness was in residence at Bum-thang, a retreat deep in the recesses of the Himalayas many days' journey from any post-office. In the second place His Highness's letters were in the language of Dharma Bhutia and in the script of Tibet, with neither of which could I claim acquaintance. For the most part I was indebted for their interpretation to M. F. von Mannen, a scholar of repute who chanced at the time to be officiating at the Imperial Library at Calcutta.

In form they were unquestionably more imposing than anything of which I was capable, though I made use of the largest sheets of official notepaper that I could lay hands on. They were inscribed on sheets of parchment invariably twenty-five inches in length, and in one case of an equal depth, and they were wrapped in silk scarves of great size and high quality. When, in due course, I received the erudite translations of M. von Mannen, I realised that greatly as my own productions fell short of those of my high-placed correspondent in the matter of form, they lagged still farther behind in the matter of style and diction. Here is an example :

Given from Bum-thang in Bhután.

(*Here followed the royal seal.*)

To the Lotus throne of the Feet. To the most excellent feet of the ocean-wide-wise ruler, perfectly rich in power and wealth, the noble, great Lord Governor Sahib of Bengal, Shri, Shri, Shri, Shri, Shri, Shri, Shri, Ro-nel-shes.

Next came an intimation that there followed below a letter from the Bhutan Rajadhara, Uggyen Wang-chuk, and that it was accompanied by greetings. The opening sentences of the letter proper referred to my "felicitous body, born out of splendour, shining exceedingly like the Lord of the Water-Crystal," *i.e.* the Moon, and proceeded as follows: "that out of love of heart we have not been rejected by the long (*i.e.* merciful) eyes at the great distance, but have received an answer to the second letter submitted before; for that kindness we also offer thanks. That the Chief Great Lord Sahib will come to our territory of Paro to travel and look round has also caused measureless gladness and joy to arise in our heart." Much more followed in the same vein, and in conclusion I was informed that the Deb Zimpon, Tobgay Dorjé, a high official of the country with whom I was already well acquainted, would be requested to accompany me during my visit. "Further, as to servant Tobgay, if there is any work in which he can serve or assist you, he must thoroughly perform it. So it is. If he is taken along to make arrangements, to act as a guide or to be of assistance, then, concerning whatever is necessary to be done, please command him to perform the service. Knowing, knowing, knowing." The meaning of these last words was that the matter was left to my discretion. And the letter concluded with the usual formula—"with a complimentary scarf as a keepsake, from Bum-thang in Bhutan"—followed by the date according to the Tibetan calendar.

The upshot of a correspondence extending over some five months was that I was in possession of a cordial invitation from His Highness to visit Bhutan, while he was apprised that I would convey to him the insignia of a Knight Grand Commander of the Order of the Indian Empire, recently conferred upon him by His Majesty. This latter item in the programme was destined, unfortunately, to remain unfulfilled. A virulent outbreak of influenza necessitated a change in His Highness's plans and prevented him at the last moment from leaving Bum-thang to meet me at Paro as he had intended.

Bhutan is altogether outside the beat of the ordinary traveller, and has been visited by comparatively few Europeans. It was with feelings of some excitement, consequently, that we started off from Darjeeling on the morning of October the 20th. Yet no amount of pleasurable anticipation could quite dispel the regret with which I was assailed on realising that I was bidding farewell to Darjeeling for the last time. There are times when one is reminded with something of a shock of the irrevocability of the past; of the inexorable fact that Time has turned his key in that lock which, once closed, can never be reopened, and that there lies behind one in the ever-expanding limbo of the past the irretrievable accumulation of all that one has thought and said and done—of all, in fact, that goes to the making of that which, in the language of the philosophy of India, is styled one's karma. And with such thoughts there came inevitably to mind the poignant words in which the Persian poet embodied, many centuries ago, the quintessence of the philosophic fatalism of the East—

The Moving Finger writes; and, having writ,
Moves on: nor all thy Piety nor Wit
Shall lure it back to cancel half a Line,
Nor all thy Tears wash out a Word of it.

* * * * * *

The first part of our journey lay over familiar ground, and we purposed wasting little time upon it as far as Chumbi. With the aid of a Ford car we covered the sixty odd miles to Gangtok by the afternoon of the 21st, and on the following day ascended nineteen miles through dense forest, passing from tree-ferns and roses to hard-bitten firs, to emerge, just as darkness was descending, on the brink of a bare mountain cup in which lay bedded the lake of Changu, set like a mirror to reflect the snow-flecked peaks surrounding it. The next day's march took us over the Nathu La (14,750 feet), which lay under two feet of snow, and across which screamed a biting wind which took the skin off our faces; and on the 24th we swung down the mountain side to Chumbi through a sparkling atmosphere laden with the aromatic scent of the forest, and over sward gay with clusters of little flowers, whose upturned cups of blue seemed to reflect something of the brilliance of the sky above.

We found our old friends the lamas of the Karjui monastery busy on the construction of a huge image of Buddha Maitreya. This is one of quite a number of these figures which have been set up in this part of the Buddhist world during the past few years, and it would almost seem as if amongst the Buddhists of the Eastern Himalayas, there is a subconscious expectation of the immanence of the Buddha that is to come. Leaving them, after inspecting some additions to the buildings since our previous visit, we were met by the Tibetan trade agent and taken by him to his residence at Pi-pi Thang, where we were regaled with luncheon.

He was a man of wide experience, and had only recently returned to a post which he had occupied many years before, at the special request of the Dalai Lama, though he had actually retired from public life when he received his orders. In the interval he had seen stirring times, and, as a general in the Tibetan army, had been three times wounded when leading his men against the Chinese in the fighting at Lhasa which led to the flight of the Dalai Lama in 1910. He now played the part of an exceedingly genial host. The meal began with the arrival of eight china bowls each containing some dainty, which we fished for with chopsticks at our pleasure. We soon discovered that this was a mere prelude which served the same purpose as does the *zakuska* at a Russian feast, namely, that of exciting in the appetite an alert anticipation of that which is to come. The body of the meal was served in larger bowls, two of which were placed in the centre of the circle formed by their smaller companions. For drink we were plied with the wine of Ssŭch'uan, a vintage highly prized by our host, to whom it had been conveyed from China in a fine stone jar. At frequent intervals one of the centre bowls was removed to be replaced by another containing some new delicacy, and in this way we were provided with the opportunity of sampling in an almost incredibly short space of time some twenty or more specimens of the culinary art of Tibet. A sure indication that the banquet was approaching its climax was the appearance of four new dishes simultaneously. The Cavalry Officer's chopsticks were hovering tentatively over a bowl containing something which had the appearance of a glucous compound. "What is that?" I asked, by way of making conversation. "Shark's stomach," came the reply. The Cavalry Officer's chopsticks switched off convulsively, after the manner of magnetic needles brought suddenly into a field of violent attraction, and dived hurriedly into another bowl. Shark's fins had appeared and been disposed of much earlier in the meal, and further samples of the animal's anatomy came somewhat unexpectedly.

New Yatung, one hundred and two miles from Darjeeling, stands in a comparatively open valley. Not far above it the mountain walls begin to close in, and at a distance of about two miles we came to a narrow defile where stand the remains of a formidable wall, built by the Chinese in the eighties of last century to bar the influx of foreigners, *i.e.* the British. On the smooth surface of the rock at one end of this barricade are some frescoes, including a brightly coloured portrait of Guru Rimpoché and his two wives, and just beyond, on a slight eminence, the ruins of Chinese barracks and official buildings. The dramatic collapse of the Chinese, paving the way for the return of the Dalai Lama which has already been referred to, seems to have been due, in part at least, to the growth of a spirit of indiscipline, amounting almost to rebellion, in the ranks of the Chinese army. In China itself revolution was in progress. In the turmoil at home the needs of a distant enterprise were lost sight of, and the necessary despatch of money and supplies was overlooked. Unpaid and uncared for, the Chinese soldiery jibbed. The officers lost control and demoralisation set in, with the result that the Tibetans came into their own again.

Beyond these ruins we came to a prosperous-looking village called Ga-lin-ka, signifying "Happy Place," and then marched for two miles or so along the edge of a narrow strip of meadow-land called Ling-ma-thang. At the far end of this grazing ground the mountains closed in finally upon the waters of the Amo-chu, and for the remainder of the day and the first part of the following day we hugged the banks of the river as it twisted through a memorable gorge, cutting immense curves between walls of naked rock which rose perpendicularly from bastions of forest-clad mountain. Three or four miles beyond Gautza, a small bungalow where we spent the night of October the 25th, we rose above the tree-line, and the scenery underwent a striking change. Cliffs and forest-clad precipices gave place to the rounded hills of the Tibetan highlands. The landscape was bare, a jumble of vast undulations garbed in browns and yellows, not the staring colours which one associates with the stark aridity of some parts of these Brobdingnagian uplands, but the dull, lifeless shades of colour which are produced by monotonous stretches of withered grass. And scattered over these rolling expanses were immense herds of bushy-tailed yaks.

The day was not to close, however, without providing yet one more sensational example of the endless variety of form and colour in which Nature, in these regions, delights to display herself. Rounding a range of hills we were suddenly faced by Cho-mo-lhari—"the Divine Queen of Mountains"—reared aloft like the glittering spire of some vast cathedral, ten thousand feet sheer above the plain; and a few minutes later Phari Jong came into sight, looking in the distance, with the village which has grown up round it, like a drab excrescence

Plate 2.

CHO-MO-LHARI, THE DIVINE QUEEN OF MOUNTAINS, 24.000 FT.

" . . . . reared aloft like the glittering spire of some vast cathedral, ten thousand feet sheer above the plain."

of the dusty plain itself. A halt of a day here gave us time to explore both the village and the surrounding country.

The stretch of country to which the village of Phari gives its name is certainly a remarkable place. It is, in fact, an inclined plain about ten miles in length, rising from 14,000 feet at its southern end to rather more than 15,000 feet at its northern extremity, where it is bounded by the Tang La. Running parallel to it on either side are ranges of bare hills, that on the east culminating in Cho-mo-lhari, whose central peak, soaring to nearly 24,000 feet, stands sentinel over the pass below. Beyond the labyrinth of desolate hills encompassing the plain on the west can be seen the snow-clad highlands of Sikhim, conspicuous amongst them a huge clump, Pawhunri, rising to 23,000 feet, and blocking out from view the stony gateway of the Donkhya La.

The Jong itself stands in the middle of the southern half of the plain, and the houses of the village, of perhaps three thousand souls, cluster dirtily round its southern bastions. As is so often the case with a people who have never been able to understand the curious obsession of the western races for exact knowledge, we obtained different answers to the same question. Thus the Elder learned that the meaning of the word Phari was "the hill made glorious," while I was assured that it was merely a contraction of the word Phag-rhi, signifying "Pig hill." It was open to us, consequently, to adopt whichever meaning appeared to us to be the more appropriate, and after picking our way through the gutters of filth—fortunately at this time of year frozen solid—and gazing into the grimy interiors of the dwelling-houses, we arrived at an unanimous conclusion upon the point. We felt, in fact, that, inadequate though the observations of the eccentric traveller, Thomas Manning, almost invariably were, his description of Phari left little for later visitors to add. His room, he noted in the amazing diary which is the only record of his remarkable journey to Lhasa in 1811 which we possess, had "dirty floors and was rather cold." He also mentioned that he was obliged to cook for himself. And pondering ruefully upon these things he summed up Phari: "Dirt, dirt, grease, smoke. Misery, but good mutton." [1]

The presence of a Bhutanese agent, and the proximity of the Tremo La leading across the frontier into Bhutan, recalled the fact that, like other border towns in other lands, Phari has been no stranger to border forays. Indeed, so serious did the clash of raid and counter-raid become towards the close of the nineteenth century, that the authorities in Tibet and Bhutan laid their heads together to devise a remedy. The outcome was an agreement, "sealed by the Ruler and Nobles of Bhutan on a date of the 8th month of the Iron-Mouse year," or, to be more explicit, in September or October of the year A.D. 1900. The preamble of this curious document

[1] *Narrative of the Journey of Thomas Manning to Lhasa*, edited by Sir Clements R. Markham. Other quotations from Mr. Manning's diary in this and the following chapters are taken from the same source.

stated that as in this degenerate time many bad people of Bhutan and of Tibet were not abiding by the laws of their respective kingdoms, and consequently there were many thieves and robbers, a permanent arrangement was now made, so that there might be no ill-feeling but always good between the kingdoms. The arrangement forbade any person of certain specified places in Bhutan to "steal property, ponies, mules, yaks, and even cloth or thread" from the people on the Tibetan side of the frontier. If any one disobeying this order was caught, he was to be tried and punished in the presence of representatives of both Governments. Further stipulations, based no doubt upon experience, were added. In the event of a robber being pursued and killed, a sum of 75 ngü-sang (about 170 rupees) was to be paid as blood money through the Phari Jongpen if due from Tibet, and through the Bhutanese agent if due from Bhutan. This stipulation concluded rather quaintly with the words "and not even a word should be said about the killing of such robbers"—the meaning being that no further claim would arise in respect of the matter.

If, on the other hand, it was the robber who killed his pursuer, the matter of the killing was to be treated as a more heinous offence. The robber was to be bound and thrown into the river with the body of the person whom he had killed. In the event of the malefactor escaping, a sum of 300 ngü-sang was to be paid as blood money "without any protest." It was also settled that if a Bhutanese trader went to Phari or Chumbi "no one must trouble him unnecessarily," and *vice versa.* The final clause of the document declared that the arrangement had been made for the good of both the Tibetan and Bhutanese "Governments, and all evil-minded people are forbidden to act as before but must abide by these conditions for ever."

It is disappointing to have to relate that an eirenicon conceived with such patent sincerity, should have failed so signally of its purpose. Writing only five years after the conclusion of the agreement, the British political officer in Chumbi reported that the subjects of the Paro Penlop in Western Bhutan had long enjoyed an unenviable reputation for raiding, and that the people of the Ha district adjoining the Chumbi valley, were usually regarded as the worst offenders of them all. And after pointing out that the only protection of the people rested on the agreement, he added that "it did not work very well: the raiding ceased for a short time but began again."

No tales of the thrust and parry of marauding bands reached our ears, and it is probable that what the agreement of 1900 failed to effect has been brought about by the enlightened rule of His Highness Sir Uggyen Wang-chuk, ably seconded by the late Bhutanese agent to Great Britain, Uggyen Raja, and his son and successor Tobgay Dorjé, whose ancestral home rears its frowning walls aloft in unchallenged ascendancy over the turbulent dwellers in the valley of the Ha.

We obtained our bird's-eye view of the country from a spot between 17,000 and 18,000 feet in altitude, on the gravelly foot-hills from which the central peak of Cho-mo-lhari rises. It is, I think, the most striking isolated peak that I have seen. The western face of the great spire of granite, so steep that no snow rests upon it, towers into a canopy of blue. A little to the south, separated from the granite spire by a huge cleft, stands a massive mountain buried deep in snow, recalling Kabru by its resemblance to the roof of a Swiss cottage tent. Gazing down from our lofty perch over a jumble of rocky spurs, we could see the summit of the Tang La, 15,200 feet, and beyond it again the salmon-pink hills of Tuna, interrupting the monotony of an otherwise featureless void.

Phari at night conjures up visions of what one imagines a lunar landscape would be like—the dominant feature being a frozen desolation. In the dry rarefied air everything stands out in hard lines, the softer tones of gentler climes being entirely lacking. Moreover, as the sun sinks, the temperature falls with something of the shocking abruptness which the scientists tell us is characteristic of the atmosphereless moon. After being sun-baked all day our teeth chattered audibly as the temperature fell to six degrees below zero (F.) at night. The people of Phari counter the cold by the suppression of all ventilation and the burning of yak dung. Alone of all the houses the dak bungalow maintains a supply of firewood, brought laboriously from the wooded slopes of Bhutan, a peculiarity which we were quick to appreciate.

It was on the eve of our departure from Phari

that we were joined by the Deb Zimpon of Bhutan, Tobgay Dorjé, the bearer of yet another letter from His Highness acquainting me of the outbreak of influenza which was causing him to change his plans. He wrote at great length and with great cordiality, expressing his delight at the knowledge that "like the cloudless sun, emitting rays for the benefit of all the subjects owing to good deeds in a former life," I was in good health. He then explained in detail how the scourge of influenza had descended upon the valleys of Eastern Bhutan and the reasons why this made it impossible for him to leave Bum-thang. And he concluded by acquainting me with the orders which he had issued to the Paro Penlop, with a view to his receiving me on his behalf. The latter official wields great power as Governor of the western half of the country, and has played a large part in the evolution of the state. So little concerning the country is generally known to the outside world, that before proceeding with an account of it as it strikes the traveller to-day, some attempt at a brief sketch of its history seems desirable.

CHAPTER XX

BHUTAN—A CENTURY AND A HALF OF HISTORY

THE early history of Bhutan is buried in an almost impenetrable obscurity. So far as the records show, it was not until 1772 that the East India Company became conscious of the existence, across its northern frontier, of a meddlesome neighbour. And their first contact with this new-found acquaintance was not calculated to excite their sympathetic interest. The first thing to arrest attention was a cry of distress from the state of Cooch Behar, whose ruler Raja Daranda Narain, together with his brother, had been carried off across the border, and their country seized, by a filibustering expedition of wild mountaineers. This was in fact the first of a long series of border forays accompanied by kidnapping, cattle-lifting, murder, and plunder, which extended over a period little short of a century, until in 1864 it was finally brought to a close by a military episode known as the Bhutan war.

Sporadic attempts to induce better relations were made in the meantime, by the despatch of missions from the authorities in India to the

Government of Bhutan itself, or to the suzerain power in Tibet. Thus the capture of Raja Daranda Narain of Cooch Behar, in 1772, led first to the despatch of a punitive expedition under a Captain Jones in the service of the East India Company, who, with the aid of four companies of Sepoys and two pieces of cannon, effected the recovery of the Raja's territory and later of the Raja himself; and subsequently to the journey of Mr. George Bogle, "a gentleman of distinguished ability and remarkable equanimity of temper," to Bhutan and thence to Tibet in 1774, when a treaty of friendship between the former country and the East India Company was effected.

Nine years later a favourable opportunity was seized by Warren Hastings, to follow up the intercourse with Tibet begun so happily by George Bogle; and Captain Samuel Turner proceeded to Bhutan, where he spent the summer of 1783, and thence to Tashi-lhumpo, the seat of the Tashi Lama, near Shigatse in Tibet. In 1811 he was followed by the eccentric traveller Thomas Manning, whose diary was given to the world many years later by Sir Clements Markham.

The next visit of which there is any record was that of an Indian official, Babu Kishen Kanta Bose, who was sent across the border by Mr. Scott, judge of Rungpur, in 1815, in the hope of effecting a settlement of the incessant disputes which were disturbing the tracts along the border. A further mission on a large scale was despatched to Punakha, the capital of Bhutan, by the East India Company in 1837, under the charge of Captain R. B. Pemberton, an officer well qualified by experience to undertake the task. During the period which had elapsed since the visit of Babu Kishen Kanta Bose, the Company had added considerably to the length of their troublesome frontier by the occupation, in 1826, of Assam. And their perplexities were added to, not merely by this increase in the field of border warfare which they had to attempt to control, but by the virulently unhealthy nature of the newly acquired tract of country running along the foot-hills of Bhutan.

During the 'thirties they were compelled to raise a special corps of men inured to the peculiar form of sickness which scourged the land, which came to be known as the Assam Sebundies. We know more of the cause of its unhealthiness to-day than was known then. It is, in fact, the haunt of a particular breed of the malaria-carrying mosquito, namely the *Anopheles listoni*, which, unlike the *Anopheles fuliginosus* of the plains, breeds not in stagnant but in the running water of mountain streams. Experiments of great interest aimed at the destruction of the larvae were undertaken recently on the Meenglas tea estate in the Bengal Duars, but a large expenditure of time and money will be required if the pest is to be eradicated.

It was by the Assam Duars that Captain Pemberton entered Bhutan. He found, however, that intercourse between the members of his mission and the people of the country was so rigorously restricted by the Bhutanese officials, that it was with the utmost difficulty that information could be collected, and he tells how "one or two Bhuteas whose visits to my native officers were supposed to be more frequent than was necessary, were bastinadoed into a salutary disgust of the inconvenient intimacy." [1]

Finally as a prelude to the Bhutan war came the mission of Sir Ashley Eden in 1863. It was the failure of his efforts to reach a friendly settlement that at last drove the Government of India to resort to force.

From information gathered by these various missions, may be pieced together all that is known of the history of Bhutan. It is not much, for, as Sir Ashley Eden observes, "in a country in which there is no ruling class, no literature, no national pride in the past or aspirations for the future, there is as a matter of course no reliable history and very little tradition." [2] Tradition as heard by Babu Kishen Kanta Bose was to the effect that some time during the seventeenth century, when the country was in the occupation of a tribe called Cooch, now inhabiting Cooch Behar, a holy man called Lam Sapto came from the north and made his appearance at Punakha. On arrival he began to play upon a kind of pipe made of a human thigh bone and to perform miracles, at which the Cooch Raja was so terrified that he disappeared with his whole family and servants underground.

[1] Report on Bhutan by Captain R. Boileau Pemberton, dated Calcutta, November 30, 1838. Further quotations of Captain Pemberton's opinions in this chapter are taken from the same source.

[2] Report on the State of Bhutan and on the Progress of the Mission of 1863–64, by the Hon. (afterwards Sir) Ashley Eden, dated Darjeeling, July 20, 1864. Further quotations of the opinions of Sir Ashley Eden in this chapter are taken from the same source.

This left the field to the stranger, who instructed such of the people as had remained above ground in his own religious faith and customs. With unexpected self-abnegation, however, he refrained from occupying the vacant throne, but sent to Lhasa for a fellow-countryman whom he made his prime minister, and who, under the title of Deb Raja, became the virtual ruler of the country. Lam Sapto himself became occupied "entirely with the cares of religion and contemplation of the deity," and under the title of Dharma Raja became the spiritual head of the country.[1] From which it will be seen that a system was evolved which affords a parallel to that obtaining in more than one country in West and East alike, where the religious hierarchy vies with the temporal government in pomp and circumstance —in the former, for example, Italy, and in the latter Nepal, and to some extent Tibet.

This version of the crigin of the state of Bhutan was checked later by Sir Ashley Eden with the aid of Tibetan manuscripts, and lost something of its picturesqueness in the process. According to this revised version Lam Sapto had a forerunner in the shape of a party of Tibetan sepoys which settled down, forming a little colony; and on his arrival—Sir A. Eden calls him Sheptoon Lapha—they invited him to become their king under the title of Dharma Raja. Far from sending to Tibet for a colleague to share with him the chieftainship, as narrated by Kishen

[1] See an *Account of Bhutan*, by Babu Kishen Kant Bose, translated by D. Scott, Esq. Further quotations of the opinions of Babu Kishen Kant Bose in this chapter are taken from the same source.

Kanta Bose, he was deposed by a later arrival, one Farchu Dupgein Sheptoon, who thenceforward ruled in his stead. Farchu Dupgein is said to have been a good and capable ruler; to have built the forts of Angdu-Forang, Punakha, and Paro; to have drawn up a code of laws for the protection of the cultivators; and to have appointed officials styled Penlops and Jong-pens to administer the country.

It was, according to this version, his successor who separated the religious functions of the ruler from the secular, and choosing the former for himself, made way for a Deb Raja to carry on the government. In course of time a council made up of a number of the chief officials came into existence, and while the Dharma Raja succeeded by incarnation, the Deb Raja was in theory elected by the council. Actual practice, however, differed widely from the theory. What seems to have happened was, that the Deb Raja became a pawn in a perpetual struggle for power waged by the two Penlops, nominally the Governors of East and West Bhutan, with headquarters at Tongsa and Paro respectively, but actually the rulers of the country. Sir A. Eden thus sums up the resulting situation:—"In practice he (the Deb Raja) is the mere nominee of whichever of the two Penlops happens for the time to be the most powerful. . . . There are generally some three or four Debs and ex-Debs in the country. The Paro Penlop nominates a Deb and places him on the throne; a few months after the Tongsa Penlop ejects him and substitutes his own puppet. He in his turn is ejected by the Paro Penlop, and so this perpetual struggle goes on and has gone on without interruption for the last fifty years."

Oddly enough, it was the Deb who in theory nominated the two Penlops. In practice they fought their way to power, and, this being so, it became in reality a case of the survival of the fittest. The man who proved himself capable of fighting his way to the post of Zimpon, or Chief Secretary to a Penlop, was of the stuff of which Penlops themselves were made, and sooner or later usually became one. "If a Penlop is hard pressed by his brother Penlop," wrote Sir A. Eden, "he very commonly promises his Zimpon that if he will get him out of the trouble, he will within a certain number of years retire in his favour. If the Zimpon finds no other way of getting promotion he either murders or deposes his master, and both the present Penlops thus mutinied and deposed their employers."

This state of affairs is confirmed by the testimony of the admirable Kishen Kanta Bose given half a century earlier. The internal broils to which he found the country subject were said by him to be due as a rule, either to the Deb Raja doing something contrary to custom, or to his remaining in office too long. And his description of the dust-up which then ensued prepares us for the stern condemnation of the manners and customs of the country, poured forth so unsparingly at a later date by both Pemberton and Eden. "When they fight with a Deb Raja, or the Penlops among themselves," he writes, "they stand at a distance and fire arrows at each other, and if one of them is killed both parties rush forward and struggle for the dead body; whichever of them succeed in getting it, they take out the liver and eat it with butter and sugar; they also mix the fat and blood with turpentine, and making candles thereof, burn them before the shrine of the deity. The bones of persons killed in war are also used for making musical pipes, and of the skulls they make beads and also keep them set in silver for sipping water at the time of the performance of religious ceremonies."

From all of which it will be seen that the really effective pieces upon the Bhutanese chess-board, have always been the two Penlops of Tongsa and Paro. The country is actually divided into nine provinces; but since two of these, the provinces of Kuru-tod and Kuru-mad, are combined for purposes of administration, there are actually eight Penlops. The academically correct transliteration of the word, which is popularly spelt either Penlow or Penlop, is Pönlob, signifying "Teacher and Pupil." In view of the part which the two outstanding Penlops of Tongsa and Paro have invariably played in the shaping of events, one may be forgiven if one scents a delicate irony in the intended significance of this title, namely, master in his own province, but servant of the Dharma and Deb Rajas in the wider sphere of the state.

The character given to the people in most of these reports is certainly not flattering, and in the case of the official class could not well be worse. A certain measure of honesty is conceded to the peasantry; but apart from this the whole people is charged with moral depravity of almost unplumbed depths. Kishen Kanta Bose declared that almost all the women prostituted themselves up to the age of twenty-five or twenty-six, and added of the people in general, that they were so full of fraud and intrigue that they would not scruple to murder their own father or brother to serve their interest. Dr. Griffiths, the medical member of Captain Pemberton's mission, who entered the country "prepossessed in favour of everything bearing the name of Bootan," declared that the women in their extreme indelicacy formed a marked contrast with such other hill tribes as he was acquainted with; and he attributed the scantiness of the population "to the custom of polyandry and one of its opposites *agamy*," to bad government, and to the "filthy and licentious habits of the people."[1] Captain Pemberton was equally emphatic. While admitting that he had observed here and there some redeeming traits of character, his final conclusion was that, much as he had travelled and resided amongst various tribes on the frontier, he had never known one "so degraded in morals as the Buteas." And Sir A. Eden's opinion coincided closely with those of Captain Pemberton and Dr. Griffiths. He found the cultivators "intelligent, tolerably honest, and, all things considered, not very untruthful." But this was the best that he could

[1] *Journal of the Mission to Bhutan in 1837–38*, by William Griffiths, Esq., M.D. Further quotations of the opinions of Dr. Griffiths in this chapter are taken from the same source.

say. In other respects his condemnation was as unequivocal as that of his predecessors. They were "immoral and indecent in their habits to an extent which almost surpassed belief," and possessed no sort of sense of shame or honour.

And if the character of the peasantry was bad, that of the officials was infinitely worse. Captain Pemberton did not hesitate to stigmatise them as "shameless beggars, liars of the first magnitude, whose most solemnly pledged words were violated without the slightest hesitation, who would play the bully and sycophant with equal readiness," and as persons who exhibited in their conduct "a rare compound of official pride and presumption with the low cunning of needy mediocrity." Sir A. Eden agreed with Captain Pemberton, and added that there were no laws except the will of the Penlops and Jong-pens. Kishen Kanta Bose had said very much the same thing fifty years before. The punishment for robbery was described by him as being confinement for six months or a year, after which the offender's property was seized and he himself sold as a slave, all his relations being liable to the same punishment. After this the punishment for murder strikes one as being comparatively light. The murderer "must pay 126 rupees to the Deb Raja and something to the other Counsellors and to the heirs of the deceased. If he cannot pay this sum he is tied to the dead body and thrown into the river." This is practically confirmed by Sir A. Eden, though the nature of the punishment depended, according to him, more upon expediency than upon the character of the crime. If a murder or robbery was committed by a man whom it was thought desirable to get rid off, his property was confiscated to the Penlop, and he himself, "his hands and feet being tied, is thrown into the river from a kind of drop." Otherwise he was merely confined until he surrendered all his property. Writing of his experiences in Bhutan early in the present century, Mr. Claude White describes the punishment for murder as the cutting off of the right hand and the severing of the tendons of the leg. And he tells us that he saw a man being taken off to undergo this punishment.

Any amount of injustice could be procured, according to Sir A. Eden, by a bribe, and an insurrection was the only remedy for an unjust decision. The result was complete administrative demoralisation, which he thought could have only one end and that at an early date—the passing of the country into other hands. And having recorded this opinion he made a not unexpected comment upon it with an obvious sigh of relief—"It is a great satisfaction to know that it cannot fall into worse hands than those of its present rulers."

Some allowance must be made for the bitterness of Sir A. Eden's attack. His mission had failed and he had been treated with the greatest indignity by persons described by a later writer—the Rev. Dr. Graham Sandberg in an article in the *Calcutta Review* for July 1898—as "ecclesiastical banditti." According to this writer one of them "took a large piece of wet barley meal out of his tea-cup and, with a roar of laughter, rubbed the paste all about Mr. Eden's face. He then pulled his hair, slapped him on the back, and indulged in several disagreeable practical jokes." Moreover, he had only succeeded in withdrawing safely from the country, after signing an agreement, the gist of which was that there should be perpetual friendship between Great Britain and Bhutan; that the former should restore to the latter all territories to which she had ever laid claim; and that a quadruple alliance should be made between Bhutan, Sikhim, Cooch Behar, and British India, under the terms of which any one of the four contracting parties being guilty of aggression against any one of the others, would be proceeded against by the other two. This remarkable document contained a thinly veiled threat. "We have written above," it stated, "that the settlement is permanent; but who knows perhaps this settlement is made with one word in the mouth and two in the heart. If, therefore, this settlement is false, the Dharma Raja's demons will, after deciding who is true or false, take his life and take out his liver and scatter it to the winds like ashes." Sir A. Eden appended his signature, but wrote beneath it "under compulsion." Small wonder.

The immediate results of the insulting treatment accorded to him were, an ultimatum from the Government of India to the Government of Bhutan; its rejection by the latter, and a declaration of war by the former. The declaration of war was embodied in a proclamation

Plate 25.

YAKS ON THE PHARI PLAIN.

"Separated from the granite spire by a huge cleft stands a massive mountain buried deep in snow."

dated November the 12th, 1864. It was stated therein that in view of the failure of Bhutan to come to an amicable settlement, in spite of constant endeavours on the part of Great Britain to bring this about, the Governor-General in Council had reluctantly resolved "to occupy permanently and annex to British territory the Bengal Duars of Bhutan and so much of the hill territory . . . as may be necessary to command the passes and to prevent hostile or predatory incursions of Bhutanese into the Darjeeling District or into the plains below."[1]

The expeditionary force advanced in two columns—one against the western and the other against the eastern half of the country—towards the end of November. All their objectives were achieved early in January 1865, and it was assumed that the Bhutanese were beaten. The assumption was too lightly made. Before the operations had been completed a manifesto in the name of the Deb Raja, addressed to the officers in command of the British troops, had made its appearance. It stated in a tone of pained surprise that he could not believe that the Queen of Great Britain had ordered the seizure of his country; further, that when two Rajas desired to fight they sent information to one another as to when the fight should begin. Such at any rate was the custom of his country. And this being so, he did not consider that they had occupied his country, since he had not

[1] *Bhutan and the Story of the Dooar War*, by Dr. Rennie. I am indebted to the same volume for the facts on which the brief narrative of the war which follows is based.

embarked upon a fight. If, however, they insisted on attacking his country without fighting he would send against them a divine force of twelve Gods who were "very ferocious ghosts." His threat was no idle one, as events were to prove; for scarcely had the British authorities decided to break up the expeditionary force when the Bhutanese, under the personal command of the Tongsa Penlop, swept down upon Dewangiri, one of the eastern posts which had been occupied, and, having cut off the water-supply, compelled its evacuation on February the 5th. Similar attacks were made with varying fortune all along the line of the occupied territory, and a complete reorganisation of the expeditionary force, including the despatch of reinforcements from Calcutta, was found necessary before the shaken prestige of British arms was re-established. Honour having been satisfied by the recapture during the spring of the posts which had been evacuated, operations remained in abeyance during the summer.

This lull in the storm was taken advantage of to attempt once more to negotiate a settlement. On June the 2nd the Viceroy, Lord Lawrence, addressed a letter to the Deb and Dharma Rajas which, after recapitulating recent events, concluded with these words: "War still continues between us. I now write again and tell you that if you really desire peace, I am ready to come to the same terms as before, but that, if you refuse, I shall now send troops still farther into your country, and shall attack you and destroy your power. If you are wise, you will attend to my letter and make peace on the conditions formerly offered. The longer you resist the worse will your condition be."

As this failed to produce the desired result, an advance into the heart of the country was decided on, and full warning given to the Deb Raja by Colonel Bruce, the political officer in charge of the negotiations, in a letter dated September the 28th, 1865. He wrote of the assembling of the British forces "to raise the purdah of the mountains," and proceeded: "If you reply quickly the army will not have moved far, but if you delay it may have reached Cherrumg, or Kenkar, or Modaka, or Chuka, before you send agents to sign a treaty; and if you delay longer still, it will have reached Wandipore, or Tongsa, or Paro, or Tassichujong and Punakha. Once set in movement it will never stop until the peace is arranged. . . . You complain that last year the war commenced too quickly; but from all my letters you will know that this year you have, at any rate, had notice for many months of what was coming."

These preparations for war at length made an impression, and in a letter to Colonel Bruce, dated October the 4th, the Deb Raja wrote: "When you speak of peace in your mouth it affords me great pleasure; but I hear that you are making roads for the passage of elephants and mules, and that sahiblogue are going backwards and forwards. Are these proper preliminary measures for making peace?" In the same letter he informed Colonel Bruce that he had ordered officers of rank to go down to treat.

The result was a treaty signed on November the 11th, 1865, the most important clause of which was that ceding to Great Britain in perpetuity, the whole of the Bengal and Assam Duars and a block of mountainous country on the left bank of the Tista river, now known as the subdivision of Kalimpong, and the grant to Bhutan by way of compensation of an annual sum rising by increments to a maximum of 50,000 rupees. In addition, free trade between the two countries was guaranteed, and the Government of Bhutan agreed to refer to the arbitration of the British Government all disputes with the rajas of Sikhim and Cooch Behar. Thus ended a century of troubled intercourse between the two countries. Henceforth the relations between Great Britain and Bhutan were to be marked by a steadily increasing cordiality.

It must be admitted that the picture given us of the country by the greater number of those who visited it during the ninety odd years preceding the Bhutan war, is a sufficiently gloomy one. Alone among them in painting the people in brighter colours were George Bogle in 1774 and Samuel Turner in 1782; and in fairness the opinion of these two observers should be given. The former spoke of the people in terms of high praise. "The more I see of the Bhutanese," he wrote, "the more I am pleased with them." He described the common people as good-humoured, downright, and, so far as he could judge, thoroughly trustworthy. Their statesmen, he declared, had "some of the art which belongs to their profession." On another occasion he paid them an even higher tribute. "The simplicity of their manners, their slight intercourse with strangers and a strong sense of religion preserve the Bhutanese from many vices to which more polished nations are addicted. They are strangers to falsehood and ingratitude." There were, however, traits of a less commendable nature which did not altogether escape him. The celibacy of a large part of the people he found to be productive of "many irregularities," and the coldness of the climate to incline them to "an excessive use of spirituous liquors." [1]

Turner came to much the same conclusion as Bogle. The lamas, he found, bound to celibacy from their first entrance into the order and interdicted "by the severest penalties from all connection with the female sex." He noted, however, that they were not denied the benefit of some friendly offices at the hands of the fair sex, and he remarked with a delightful *naïveté* that the prettiest women he saw "were employed in carrying water into the palace." He also confessed that though it was somewhat to their discredit, yet impartiality obliged him to own that his new friends were "far from having any very nice notions of cleanliness." [2]

Comparing these various accounts carefully with one another, one has little difficulty in perceiving that if the earlier writers displayed a tendency to lay stress upon the good points of the people and to gloss over certain of their

[1] *Narrative of the Mission of George Bogle to Tibet*, edited by Sir Clements Markham.

[2] *Account of an Embassy to the Court of the Teshu Lama in Tibet*, by Captain Samuel Turner.

less creditable characteristics, the later observers, drawing their conclusions under less favourable circumstances, viewed all that they saw through glasses distorted by the lack of success of their respective missions. And one has little difficulty in drawing an intelligible mean between accounts which at first sight appear irreconcilable.

So far as statesmanship is concerned, the war of 1864, followed by the treaty of 1865, proved a turning-point in the history of the country and ushered in a period of regeneration.

Sir A. Eden's conclusion had been that conditions were such that it was "quite impossible" that there could be a Government in the country "sufficiently strong to warrant an expectation that they will ever become good neighbours." His conclusion has, happily, been falsified by events, for, with the exception of a raid in the neighbourhood of Buxar in 1880 and certain outrages in the Kamrup district of Assam in 1889, which led to a temporary withholding of the subsidy and the establishment of a police station at Kakolabari, Great Britain has had no cause for complaint; but on the contrary has found in His Highness Sir Uggyen Wangchuk, now Maharaja of Bhutan, a friend and admirer and in his people most excellent neighbours.

The particularly cordial relations now existing between Great Britain and Bhutan date from the beginning of the present century, when history took a curious turn. For just as in 1772, when the people of Bhutan had been guilty of an incursion into the territory of Cooch

Behar, the Government of Tibet played the part of mediators between Bhutan and ourselves, so now, at the dawn of the twentieth century, when the people of Tibet had been guilty of repeated violations of the frontier of Sikhim, the Government of Bhutan worked earnestly to bring about a settlement between Tibet her erstwhile suzerain, and Great Britain her former enemy. In 1899 the Bhutanese agent, Uggyen Kazi, was employed to write a letter to the Dalai Lama on his own account, representing the desirability of his deputing an official to meet the representatives of Great Britain to discuss questions affecting trade and the frontier. Nothing coming of this attempt, Uggyen Kazi was commissioned by Lord Curzon to convey a letter from himself to the Dalai Lama. This venture was equally unsuccessful, and in August 1901 the envoy returned with the letter unopened. The attitude of Bhutan became of real importance when the British mission, which was eventually to find its way to Lhasa, marched up the Chumbi valley to Tuna at the beginning of 1904. For Bhutan lay, a potential danger, upon the flank of its attenuated line of communication. In February the Trimpuk Jong-pen crossed the Tremo La from Bhutan to Phari and proceeded to Tuna, where Colonel Younghusband was in camp. He proved a sensible man and a firm friend, and promised the whole-hearted support of his country.

Later on in June the British envoy was met by a Bhutanese official of higher rank and of much greater importance. This was no less a man than

Uggyen Wang-chuk, the Penlop of Tongsa, round whose personality the history of Bhutan during the past forty years may be said to centre. He used his utmost influence to bring about an agreement. The Tibetans themselves turned to him when they realised that Great Britain was at last in earnest, and in July the Dalai Lama wrote to him asking his mediation, adding somewhat quaintly: "Will you also request the English privately not to nibble up our country."[1] After the arrival of the British in Lhasa, he himself proceeded there and proved of the greatest assistance in carrying through the negotiations, which were crowned by the Anglo-Tibetan Convention of September the 7th, 1904. These services were rewarded in due course when Mr. White proceeded to Bhutan as the representative of His Majesty in 1905, to convey to him the insignia of a Knight Commander of the Indian Empire.

Circumstances deprived me of the pleasure of meeting him, but those few Englishmen who have done so have been unanimous in their praise of his character and his attainments. He first came to the front as an exceptional personality when, in 1885, being then little more than a lad of twenty-four years, he rose in wrath against a faction headed by the Tassi-chu Jong and Punakha Jong-pens, who, trading upon his youth, had kept back from him his lawful share, as Tongsa Penlop, of the British subsidy. The successful outcome of this venture established him firmly as a power in the land. Twenty

[1] *India and Tibet*, by Sir Francis Younghusband, K.C.S.I., K.C.I.E.

years later circumstances conspired to throw authority into his hands. The Dharma Raja had died and no reincarnation had been discovered. The Deb Raja, in accordance with custom under such circumstances, held both offices, and being by nature disposed towards a life of meditation, became a recluse, devoting himself wholly to the spiritual affairs of the country. The control of things temporal fell naturally into the hands of the strong man, and the strong man without question was the Tongsa Penlop. The recognition accorded to him by the British Government further consolidated his position, and at the great public ceremony at Punakha, at which the insignia of his knighthood in the Order of the Indian Empire were conferred upon him, Mr. Claude White described the "almost interminable procession" of those who paid him homage and made him gifts: "heaps of tea, bags of rice and Indian corn, fabrics—silk, woollen, and cotton—of all colours and values, with little bags of gold dust and rupees appearing at the top."[1]

In 1905 Sir Uggyen received and accepted an invitation to visit Calcutta on the occasion of the visit of His Majesty, then Prince of Wales, and he returned to Bhutan with an appreciation, derived from personal experience, of the wider world which lay beyond his own mountain gateways.

The crowning event in the evolution of the state came the following year when, on December the 17th, 1907, the man who had guided his

[1] *Sikhim and Bhutan*, by J. Claude White, C.I.E.

country so successfully through twenty eventful years was installed as hereditary Maharaja of the country. No greater testimony to the position which he had acquired amongst his countrymen could be found than in the contents of the parchment scroll, on which was inscribed the oath of allegiance taken by the chiefs and headmen of Bhutan on the occasion. A translation published by Mr. White, who was present at the ceremony, reads as follows :

To the Foot of the Two-fold Judge :

Most Respectfully Prayeth,

There being no Hereditary Maharaja over this State of Bhutan, and the Deb Rajah being elected from amongst the Lamas, Lopons, Councillors, and the Chiolahs of the different districts, with all the subjects, having discussed and unanimously agreed to elect Sir Uggyen Wang-chuk, Tongsa Penlop, the Prime Minister of Bhutan, as Hereditary Maharaja of this State, have installed him, in open Durbar, on the golden throne on this the 18th day of the 11th month of Sa-tel year, corresponding to the 17th December 1907, at Poonakha-phodang.

We now declare our allegiance to him and his heirs with unchanging mind, and undertake to serve him and his heirs loyally and faithfully to the best of our ability. Should any one not abide by this contract by saying this and that, he shall altogether be turned out of our Company.

In witness thereto we affix our seals.

The same authority, who was present at a number of discussions between the newly elected Maharaja and his Council during the immediately succeeding days, has told us of the sincerity with which problems of education, of trade, and of the possible developments of the natural resources of the country were debated. All recognised that the great obstacle in the way of progress was lack of funds, and a decision was arrived at to move the Government of India in the matter. The outcome was a treaty signed on January the 8th, 1910, whereby the annual allowance of Rs.50,000 made by Great Britain to Bhutan was increased to Rs.100,000 from January of that year; Great Britain again pledging herself to exercise no interference in the internal administration of Bhutan; and the Bhutanese Government agreeing to be guided by the advice of the Government of Great Britain in regard to its external relations.

In December 1911 His Highness attended the great durbar held by His Majesty the King Emperor at Delhi, and received further recognition in the shape of a Knight Commandership of the Order of the Star of India. And during the great world war His Highness gave tangible proof of his desire to render to Great Britain such aid as his state was capable of. By his internal policy, an example of which in the matter of education will be given later, he has given evidence of his desire to improve the lot of those over whom he has been chosen to rule. He has, indeed, proved himself a worthy recipient of the greater honour which has now been conferred upon him, the badge of which I was only prevented by an accident from investing him with in person.

CHAPTER XXI

INTO A MEDIAEVAL WORLD

Our departure from Phari was picturesque. We were accompanied for the first mile or so by the whole of the official, and part of the unofficial, population of the town. The former was dressed in its brightly coloured official robes, and all were mounted on ponies, donkeys, or mules. There was no particular track, and we scurried helter-skelter towards the hills on the east of the town, along the watershed of which runs the boundary between Tibet and Bhutan.

At the foot of the ascent proper there ensued a ceremonious leave-taking, after which we climbed unattended to the summit of the Tremo La, a bleak and windy spot thrust up 16,500 feet above a jumbled world of mountains, gaunt and thirsty on one side, wooded and well-watered on the other. Immediately in front of us, dominating the landscape, was a majestic snow-topped peak rising from a deep abyss to a height of 21,240 feet, called by the people of Bhutan Cho-tra-ké, "the Lord of the Cleft Rock." The track down the far side of the pass dropped steadily for some miles and then entered a stupendous gorge, through which the upper waters of the Pa-chu force their way to the lower valleys of Bhutan. For a distance of two or three miles the river rushes tumultuously down a series of waterfalls and cataracts. The track follows suit, a stony stairway of abrupt descents and cork-screw turns, down which one pitches perilously at a speed dictated by necessity rather than suggested by convenience. Here we passed into the forest zone once more, and as we descended vegetation increased rapidly in variety and wealth. Camp was pitched seven thousand feet below the pass amidst larch, spruce, and mountain oak, with lovely views both up and down the valley.

Soon after leaving camp on the morning of the 29th we came across the first specimen of Bhutanese architecture which we had seen, a massive cantilever bridge with stone towers at each end through which one passed on to a covered-in roadway, mules, ponies, and pedestrians jostling one another as they went in and out through the narrow doorways. On the far side was the abode of a minor official who collected tolls on the passing traffic and was held responsible for the upkeep of the bridge. And with our passage through the bridge, behold a curious transformation. For just as Alice, when she walked through the looking-glass, found herself in a new and whimsical world, so we, when we crossed over the Pa-chu, found ourselves, as though caught up on some magic time machine fitted fantastically with a reverse, flung back across the centuries into the feudalism of a mediaeval age.

We did not immediately realise what had

happened; but we were not long in doing so, for seven or eight miles down the valley we came upon an ancient feudal castle, whose towers and battlements frowned down upon our path from the summit of a low spur, thrown out from the main range on the right bank of the river. Duggye Jong, owing to the accident of its having escaped being burned down, shares with Simtoka Jong the reputation, which the latter enjoys for the same reason, of being the oldest in the country. It is a huge and massive building, which sprawls aimlessly over the ground, its lay-out having been determined, apparently, solely by the contours of the site on which it stands. Running down from the main building to the foot of the spur, was a passage-way enclosed by high walls and interrupted at intervals by towers of defence, the uppermost round, the centre one rectilinear, and the lowest round again. This system of outworks, corresponding roughly to the barbican of a castle of twelfth-century England, was connected with the main building by a subterranean passage.

The approach to the main fort zigzags up the hill on the south and, after passing a large chorten on a stone platform, ascends by a flight of steps to a massive entrance which constitutes the gate-house. Once through this we found ourselves in an outer courtyard of large dimensions lined on each side with stalls for mules and ponies, the obvious counterpart of the *bailey* of the castles of mediaeval England. At the far end was another immense doorway, on either side of which were guard-rooms; and

Plate 20.

DUGGYE JONG, A FEUDAL CASTLE OF BHUTAN.

beyond this again another large courtyard of irregular shape formed by the inner walls of the large three-storied buildings which constituted the main part of the castle. Facing one as one entered this inner yard, and at some little distance from one, was a broad flight of stone steps, and from the natural platform to which these gave access rose a lofty oblong tower, the dominating feature of the whole building. One recognised in this the *keep* of its English prototype. A few trees grew irregularly from chinks in the stone-flagged floor, mostly leafless, but amongst them two evergreens, the almond tree of Bhutan. Here and there ladder-like stairways gave access to the balconies that ran round the upper stories.

The rooms with their panelled walls were dark and contained little in the way of furniture. Amongst them were two chapels with the usual images, altars, and book-shelves, and from one of these a small balcony containing a huge bell projected over the valley below. This was tolled daily at 4 A.M.—so we were told—to call the villagers to their work. From chapel we proceeded to the castle storeroom, a large, rambling barn stacked with sacks of grain, bins of raw wool, cheeses and other produce; for the villagers, whose farmsteads lie scattered over the valley bottom, under the protection of the castle, pay their dues in kind. Finally, we were conducted by the keeper of the castle to the chief living-room and centre of its activities.

Room and keeper were exactly what one expected of them. The latter, a cheery and, I fear, a bibulous Friar Tuck, was the embodiment of the spirit of the age to which we had been transported. In appearance he was solid, like his castle. His head was ponderous and was supported by a goitrous neck rising from a massive frame. There was a puckish twinkle in his eye. On the dark-panelled walls of his sanctum hung rows of archaic weapons, swords, and shields. There was a little shrine before which he told his beads and gabbled his musty incantations, and, slung from a hook in a convenient corner, was an immense flagon of the horn of the Mithan, with well-polished brass mountings, the receptacle of some kind of spirituous liquor. A wooden balcony projected from the wall, the sheer drop from which to dizzy depths below would have done credit to the fall from the upper story of a New York sky-scraper. Our host squatted on a low couch issuing orders to a stalwart wench—his daughter—who in turn hustled a small crowd of retainers, with the result that before long we were being entertained royally with Tibetan tea, parched rice, fruit, and walnuts.

Back in the inner courtyard once more, we were shown a small mound from which now grows a tree, marking the spot where the vanguard of an invading expedition from Tibet had once mined the walls of the fort. The enterprise had failed, for the defenders, discovering the stratagem in time, had lain in wait and dealt with their enemies one by one in the darkness of the night, as they made their appearance at the tunnel's mouth. We camped for the night a mile or so below the jong.

Opposite to our camp, across the river, was a bay in the range of mountains which forms the eastern wall of the valley. The background of this aperture was a striking feature in the landscape, for immense cliffs of black and yellow rock rose perpendicularly in a frame of steep and heavily wooded spurs. For many hundreds of feet they rose in naked grandeur, too steep for even the tenacious vegetation of Bhutan to obtain a foothold. They would have arrested attention of themselves; but here the handiwork of Nature had been added to by man. Three-quarters of the way up, a crack, roughly horizontal, had occurred in this formidable wall, produced, one must suppose, by geologic pressure in a distant past, and in this crack the persevering priesthood of the country—the most undaunted builders, surely, that the world can show—had constructed a most surprising series of buildings.

Climbing steeply up the wooded spur on the north of the bay for a full two hours, we reached one end of this crack at a height shown by our instruments to be 2400 feet above the valley bottom, and following a narrow pathway came to the monastery, a cluster of buildings, in the architecture of which could be perceived a strong Chinese influence, clinging literally to the face of the rock. No one could give us any credible account of their origin, of the date of their construction, or of those who builded them; and we had perforce to rest content with the story told us, that Guru Rimpoché himself had come to this sublime spot riding on a tiger and had ordered the erection of the temples. And as conclusive evidence of the truth of this tradition we were referred to the name of the place—"Tak Thsang," "the Tiger's Nest." Clambering about in the series of buildings, we found the walls consisting sometimes of the face of the rock itself, sometimes of rough stone caked over with a veneer of baked earth. Other parts of the building were of wood. One portion of the series overtopped another as the fault in the face of the cliff slanted irregularly upwards, connected with one another sometimes by flights of stone steps, sometimes by more perilous wooden ladders. There were four or five main buildings in all, exclusive of connecting galleries and balconies. These latter, built of wood and projecting from the windows, overhung the cliff, which fell away sheer for two thousand feet into the abyss below.

In the topmost chamber of this strange abode, we inadvertently intruded upon a lama leading a life of solitary meditation. The intrusion must have been a disturbing incident in his dreamy existence, for in the whole previous history of Tak Thsang only two Europeans were known to have visited it. On the smooth face of the rock above the buildings we noticed a well-executed fresco containing figures, amongst which appeared to be that of Buddha; and some little distance away in a vertical cleft in the cliff was an isolated retreat, little more than a wooden cage, pinned somehow to the face of the rock, the home of some eccentric hermit.

A little to the north, on the very summit of

Plate 27. TAK THSANG, A FAMOUS MONASTERY OF BHUTAN.

a wooded peak rising to a sharp point, stood another monastery rejoicing in the name of Sang-thog Palri—an earthly copy of the famous paradise in which Guru Rimpoché is supposed to dwell. We scrambled up to it and were amply rewarded for our trouble, for the site was one of marvellous beauty, commanding far-reaching views both up and down the valley of the Pa-chu. The space was too small to admit of a large building, but the shrine was a gem, and the frescoes on the walls were particularly striking, the colours, especially the greens and the golds, being wonderfully soft. In front of one of the images above the altar—presumably the god of luck—was a tray containing three bone dice. I was invited to make offerings to the deity and to throw the dice. I did so, and curiously enough threw three "ones," a throw which was immediately proclaimed by the presiding lama to be supremely lucky! On the floor in front of the altar was the imprint of two human feet, those, we were told, of a holy lama now dead, wrought by the constancy with which he stood praying before the altar. I cannot explain the phenomenon. The floor was of wood, hard and polished by the use of ages; yet the imprint of the fore part of the foot and toes was as perfect as if it had been taken in wax, something quite different from most of the famous footprints of the world—such, for example, as that on the rock at the top of Adam's Peak in Ceylon, which bears no resemblance to a human foot at all.

Before descending we obtained a view of a

number of other monastic buildings crowning the surrounding heights. It is difficult to estimate the time and labour which must have been devoted to carrying material to these remote and in some cases almost inaccessible spots, and then erecting these immense piles of buildings. No records seem to have been preserved — if, indeed, any were ever made—and their construction remains a riddle on a par with that of the pyramids of Gizeh.

Camp was pitched a little lower down the valley, leaving a short march of five or six miles to Paro, the chief centre of population and headquarters of the Penlop, or Governor of Western Bhutan. And it was our entry into Paro that finally brought home to us the era into which we had unwittingly stumbled. So far as we could judge it corresponded with extraordinary faithfulness to that of feudal England, or at any rate of feudal England as it has been pictured for us by the pen of Sir Walter Scott. With dawn the camp became the scene of an unwonted stir. This was occasioned by the arrival of a guard sent out by the Penlop to escort us into his capital; and the most cursory inspection satisfied us that if mediaeval ceremonial was to be the order of the day, no escort could have been better chosen. Those composing it wore spherical helmets of burnished metal which flashed in the rays of the sun, and from which a curtain of brightly coloured cloth fell down as a protection to ears and neck. For the rest they were attired in togas of Chinese silk brocade caught up at the waist with a girdle, whence they fell loosely to the knee. The colours of these garments were as varied as they were vivid—blues of the brightest turquoise and the deepest sapphire, rose pinks, scarlets, plums, greens and yellows. Carried slung across the back were a circular shield of buffalo hide with bosses of metal representing sun, moon, and stars, and two long straight swords. Attached to this brilliantly attired throng were two trumpeters in scarlet, recalling, for some inexplicable reason, the knave of hearts of a pack of ordinary playing-cards, and two dancers in blue with cross belts of white and scarlet, wearing forage-caps with long coloured streamers and carrying in each hand small hand-drums.

In due course a procession was formed, and we sallied forth with a pomp and circumstance befitting the occasion. At the head of the cavalcade marched twenty helmeted warriors, swords swinging and helmets glittering. Next came the two trumpeters, who blew a fanfare from time to time giving warning of our approach. Behind them tripped the dancers, who brought the whole procession to a halt whenever they came to a piece of ground which they deemed suitable for the treading of a measure. Next marched four members of the particular detachment which had been detailed to act as my personal bodyguard — well-set-up men wearing cloth head-dresses and purple blouses above striped kilts. I rode immediately behind them on a gaily caparisoned mule led by a syce in scarlet, and followed by more members of the bodyguard. The procession proper ended with the Elder, the Cavalry Officer, and the British trade agent from Gyangtse, who in the absence of the Sardar Bahadur, who was unhappily detained on duty elsewhere, had accompanied us from Yatung. But as we moved slowly down the valley we attracted to ourselves the population of such villages as chanced to lie upon our route. The whole ride to Paro was, in fact, dramatic beyond our wildest expectations, and must have provided just such a spectacle as did the concourse of knights and their squires which made its way to the meadow at Ashby-de-la-Zouche, made famous by the deeds of chivalry of Ivanhoe, Le Noir Fainéant, and other goodly knights.

Some little distance away from Paro we came upon a gaily bedecked tent by the road-side, and here, awaiting us, were the Paro Penlop and the Jong-pen of Punakha with their retainers. Scarves of welcome were presented and tea and rice served, and after a suitable interval we proceeded to the semi-permanent camp which had been prepared for us on a wide stretch of level ground, immediately below a limestone bluff from which frowned down upon us the battlements of Paro Jong. Alighting here at a splendidly appointed durbar shamiana, we were entertained once more, this time with three different kinds of beverage served in succession, followed by twelve varieties of fruit brought in one after the other in pretty Bhutanese baskets. The first of the beverages was a compound of milk, sugar, yak-cheese, and some root, the name of which I was unable to ascertain; the second consisted of milk and saffron, and the third of Bhutan tea. Amongst the fruits I identified melon, persimmon, Bhutan raisin, oranges, pears, and pan and betel nut. In a screened courtyard forming an ante-room to the main tent was a huge cauldron filled with the beer of the country. A ladleful was handed to me, which I touched and which was then returned to the cauldron. This brought the ceremony of welcome to an end, and we were at liberty to retire to our respective quarters.

But the ceremonial of the day was not yet concluded, and a further function of great picturesqueness took place in the afternoon, the chief item in which was the exchange of gifts between the Maharaja and myself. Fortunately in expectation of an investiture we had brought uniforms with us, or we should have cut poor figures in the pageant in which we found ourselves the central figures. A gathering of officials, soldiers, retainers of every description, and lamas—of these latter some in robes of black and some of red—assembled in the durbar-tent. A procession was then formed of the Penlop and ourselves, and we proceeded at a slow march, the measured tread of which was set religiously by the Cavalry Officer and as religiously upset by the Elder, to take our place in the centre of the assembly. The walls of the tent were hung with magnificent banners, some embroidered, some painted, and with the curious umbrella-shaped ornaments that one sees in some of the temples. On either side of us were groups of lamas and officials, while the courtyard was massed with the gaily clad members of the escort, the whole presenting a wonderful feast of colour. The gifts of the Maharaja were then formally presented by the Penlop —finely chased swords and a shield and helmet, Bhutan cloth and Chinese silks, and finally a pawing Bhutanese stallion, which was led champing fiercely at its bit up to the entrance of the tent.

This latter was, I think, a specimen of the breed of mountain pony called Tangun, of which Turner gave a detailed description in the account of his journey through Bhutan in 1783. His first encounter with one left a deep impression upon his mind, for he had scarcely entered the mountains when he met " a led Tangun horse which came neighing and prancing with such impetuosity that I expected he would have engaged the Zeenkaub's more pacific animal." Thereafter he was evidently at some pains to acquaint himself with the characteristics of the breed, for he gives a long account of it, laying stress upon the strength of limb which is developed as a result of the perpetual climbing of steep mountains. " Accustomed to struggle against opposition," he tells us, " they seem to inherit this spirit as a principle of their nature ; and hence they have acquired a character amongst Europeans of being headstrong and ungovernable ; though in reality it proceeds from an excess of eagerness to perform their task." This charitable view of the exuberance of spirit of the Tangun horse is discounted to some extent by the naïve admission which follows it : " indeed some of those that come into our

Plate 28.

THE KEEP OF DUGGYE JONG.

"Facing one as one entered this inner yard rose a lofty oblong tower, the dominating feature of the whole building."

hands aged, have acquired habits of resistance which it is rather difficult to modify or reform." [1] The Tangun horse's claim to greatness does not rest wholly on his characteristics, however. He has figured in history, for it was laid down in the treaty of 1774 that for possession of a small piece of territory named Chichakotta, the Deb Raja should pay an annual tribute to the East India Company of five Tangun horses.

With the presentation of my return presents the more formal part of the programme was completed, and we moved off to a green behind the camp to witness a display of archery. A large crowd of spectators had come in from the country-side for many miles around. Amongst them we recognised the faces of many whom we had already met, and in particular that of Friar Tuck of Duggye Jong, who, with his buxom daughter, had descended from his mountain fastness bent upon enjoying the fun. He was a portly and a jovial figure as he strutted to and fro, making free use of a witty tongue, to judge by his expression, and chewing much betel-nut the while. Locksley had his counterpart in a skilled bowman who had come down from Bumthang to take part in the contest. Small targets were fixed at each end of a pitch of about a hundred and twenty paces. After releasing their shafts the archers shouted wildly at them, adjuring them to fly true to the mark. This practice was soon seen to be necessary, though on this

[1] *Account of an Embassy to the Court of the Teshu Lama in Tibet*, by Captain Samuel Turner. Other quotations from Turner in this and the succeeding chapter are taken from the same source.

occasion it proved, unhappily, to be of little effect, though, to the huge and obviously surprised delight of the onlookers, one shaft did at length find the target just before dusk descended and brought the proceedings to a close.

CHAPTER XXII

PARO JONG

WE spent the greater part of a day in a visit to Paro Jong. It is difficult to speak dispassionately of the architectural merits of the building. One is overwhelmed by its immensity, and one's critical faculties are swamped by the one dominant impression which it leaves upon one's mind —that of size. Other ideas are chased away by ideas of mere measurement. One's first thought is that here one is confronted by a thing of vast conception; and one's succeeding thoughts are all subject to the tyranny of this same idea.

It stands solidly on the summit of a rocky bluff overlooking the river, a vast quadrilateral with a stout buttress thrown out on the north-west side. So far as I could estimate, the actual building covers an area three hundred feet in length by a hundred and fifty feet in breadth. The bluff drops perpendicularly to the river; but the building itself stands back some paces from the south-west edge where a stone-flagged plinth, hemmed in by a semicircular battlemented wall flush with the fall of the cliff, forms a terrace. The walls of this huge quadrilateral suggest two ideas—height and mass. They tower above one, huge spaces of white-washed stone, surmounted, beneath the large overhanging eaves of a pent-house roof, by a broad band of dull red pierced by a row of narrow windows.

As is the case with most of the jongs in Bhutan, the existing building is of recent date, the greater part of it having been erected a dozen or more years ago upon the smouldering ruins of its predecessor. Those who built it seem to have followed faithfully upon the lines of the building which it replaced, for Turner's description of the jong as he saw it in 1783 gives a fairly accurate picture of the castle as one sees it to-day. He, too, was impressed by its size and solidity, for he asserts that "the castle, or palace of Paro . . . is constructed and the surrounding ground laid out more with a view to strength and defence than any place I have seen in Bhutan." The main entrance is at the north-east end of the building and is approached along a stone-flagged causeway terminating in a flight of stone stairs, at the top of which stands its immense doorway.

From our camping ground we crossed the river by a double-towered, covered-in bridge over which must have passed at intervals, more than a century before, Bogle, Turner, and Manning. It is, in fact, referred to by the last two, Turner comparing it to other bridges of a similar type of which he had given a description, Manning finding in it a subject for one of the vacuous comments with which his diary abounds. "In riding over the lofty bridge into Paro," he jots down, "if the horse curvets, it must

Plate 20.

TAK THSANG, THE TIGER'S NEST.

"And in this crack the persevering priesthood of the country had constructed a most surprising series of buildings."

go slap down thirty feet into the rocky, stony stream." Without suggesting a reason he proceeds, "but that danger is imaginary." It was imaginary in all probability because, as Turner remarked in 1783, "the bridge over the Patchieu is covered in the same manner as those of Tassisudon and Punnakha and has two spacious gateways"—a description which applies to this day. With typical inconsequence Manning adds, without a pause, "I could not persuade them to give me any fish."

No complaints of this sort troubled us as we wound picturesquely up the steep side of the bluff, to be welcomed at the castle gate-house by the Penlop. Standing framed in the massive wooden doorway he presented a remarkable picture. For his age—he was said to be nineteen or possibly twenty at the time of our visit—he is of amazing proportions, of no great height but of almost incredible breadth and thickness, and with limbs of extraordinary size. A small, flat nose and long and very narrow eyes set in a large, round face, with a complexion tending towards pink, the whole framed in a mass of long and very thick black hair, suggested the presence of a strong strain of Mongolian blood.

Passing through the gate-house, we entered the north-eastern half of a huge courtyard formed by the inner walls of the main building. From the centre of this enclosure rises a colossal tower of many stories tapering slightly up to a pagoda-like roof, and dividing the whole enclosure roughly into two halves. Leaving this tower, round the base of which at the height of a man's shoulder we noticed a series of mani-wheels—so that he who passed by might pray—on our right, we descended a flight of steps and found ourselves in the south-west portion of the building. The rooms and verandahs which open on to three sides of this lower court are occupied by a hundred and fifty lamas, those lying on the other side of the central tower being occupied by the Penlop and his retainers, the total population of this vast baronial castle being approximately three hundred souls. The central tower consists of a series of chapels one above another, each with its complement of images and altars, and all with walls elaborately ornamented with frescoes in the conventional style of Tibet. Even these do not bring the number of chapels to an end, for in the north-west wing of the lamas' quarters is a noble pillared hall ninety feet square, which gives access to a chancel containing a gigantic altar, above which gazes down, with that expression of sublime repose which is familiar to all who are acquainted with the imagery of Buddhism, a sitting figure of the Master some twenty feet in height. The great square pillars of this remarkable hall are carved and painted—as are also the walls—with thousands of figures of Buddha and of the gods and demi-gods of Bhutan and Tibet.

Once in the year an elaborate display of pantomimic dancing is given, and once in the year certain embroidered banners of great size and striking workmanship are unfurled. In honour of our visit this annual celebration had this year been fixed for November the 1st, and as

Plate 30.

MEMBERS OF OUR BHUTANESE ESCORT.

". . . . if mediæval ceremonial was to be the order of the day, no escort could have been better chosen."

we approached the far end of the lower courtyard we saw the banners, three in number, hanging on the wall of a wide verandah each covering a space of some twelve feet by eight. Here seats had been provided for us, and for the next two hours we witnessed a corybantic performance of a kind with which we were now tolerably familiar; but the dresses were, if anything, more gorgeous and the masks more bizarre than any that we had hitherto seen. The dance of the spirits of the graveyard carried one off to a gruesome world of ghouls and vampires; the black hat dance of twenty performers, to a land of gorgeous colour and elaborate design; while a procession and stately measure by the "mild deities" arrested attention by reason of the aprons of lace-work made of beads of bone, which were worn by the performers over robes of beautiful Chinese silk brocade. Scene succeeded scene, working up to a dramatic finale of over eighty dancers, the creations, one could only imagine, of a mind lost in the spectral abysses of acute delirium—inhabitants of a world half animal, half human, biped stags, monkeys, elephants, hawks, and parrots pirouetting and curtseying to kindred monsters for which human language provides no names.

The whole corybantic drama was admirably staged in the lower courtyard, affording an open space of approximately eighty feet by sixty. The verandahs and two great galleries running round two of the three stories of the building were packed with people in holiday attire, and from first to last the performance was carried on to the accompaniment of the eerie refrain which the people of these wild mountains produce with such striking effect from their enormous trumpets and their cymbals, horns, and drums. Outstanding amongst the instruments on this occasion was a magnificent pair of silver trumpets ten feet in length. At the joints they were embellished with elaborate gold mountings, the whole being the gift of Uggyen Raja and his son. A lighter touch was given to this strange performance by the capers and interjections of a comically masked clown—the obvious counterpart of Wamba, the son of Witless, jester to Cedric the Saxon—whose sallies appealed irresistibly to the sense of humour of the crowd.

Before leaving the jong we were bidden to the Penlop's own quarters in the east of the building. Here in a pillared room, the walls of which were decorated with brightly coloured frescoes and hung with large numbers of archaic guns, swords, shields, quivers of arrows, and other weapons, we were entertained at a Bhutanese meal consisting of tea, rice, yak's meat, eggs, and other dishes which we failed to identify, sour milk and Bhutanese beer. No one could have been more cordial than our host the Penlop, and nothing could have provided a more striking contrast than the attitude of the Bhutanese officials as a whole, compared with the behaviour of their forerunners towards the British envoys of the century before.

There was one other building at Paro which could not fail to arrest attention. This was a huge chorten standing at the foot of a mountain

Plate 31.

A PERFORMER IN A CORYBANTIC DRAMA.

"The dresses were, if anything, more gorgeous and the marks more bizarre than any that we had hitherto seen."

spur on a tongue of land formed by the junction of a tributary stream with the Pachu. It attracted attention both on account of its size, and also by reason of the fact that in shape it followed the chortens of Sikhim and Tibet with their curved outline, whereas the architecture of Bhutan for the most part runs to straight lines and avoids curves. Closer inspection showed that it possessed a further peculiarity—it was, in fact, a chorten within a chorten. The space between the shell and the core was in pitch darkness; but the light of a candle showed that the walls were covered with elaborate paintings, an offering made by the artist solely to the glory of God. This, as the Elder put it, was surely "a wonderful conception." The history of the construction of the building, as narrated by the people of Paro, was more wonderful still. In the first place it was the end of a chain of buildings, running along a mountain range to a bridge at Chakung ferry across the Sanpo in Tibet. But it served a more useful purpose. The builder, a famous lama, on coming to Paro found the hand of death heavy upon the people of the valley. By virtue of his miraculous powers he divined the cause. A monster of the mountains, a ghoulish frog, which battened on human blood, had made its abode in the valley. The monster's mouth was detected in a hole in the ground, and was effectually stopped by the erection over it of a chorten. This was the core. In later days a rich man came along and protected the monument, whose preservation was of such vital importance to the people of Paro, by encasing it in an outer covering, "and so," as the Elder naïvely remarked, "the people of Paro were saved."

The time had now come for us to turn our steps south in the direction of the plains of Bengal. The first stage of the homeward journey was across a high range separating the Paro and the Ha valleys, a stage which we accomplished comfortably in two days. As we climbed the steep mountain side we obtained a series of wonderful views. First was a bird's-eye picture of the vale of Paro. From our point of vantage we saw how, below the junction of the Tho-chu with the Pa-chu, the valley opened out, giving space for a broad plain. Looked down on from above, this resembled a chessboard of cultivated fields with scattered, square-built houses for pieces. Here and there little groups of people were treading out the rice on smooth threshing-floors, half-a-dozen busy with their feet doing the work which was done by oxen on the threshing-floor of Araunah the Jebusite, and others binding up the sheaves of straw. On its bluff above the river Paro Jong stood out in isolated magnificence, and stretching away above it on the mountain side could be seen a thin winding thread—the road which climbs up over the Bela Pass on its way to another great feudal stronghold, Tassi-chu Jong, the home of the Dharma Raja and summer capital of the country. Three thousand feet above the valley bottom we came to Gorina, a monastery prettily situated amongst the trees, and camped comfortably for the night a few miles farther on in the shelter of a forest of larch.

Plate 32

THE PARO VALLEY.

"Looked down on from above this resembled a chess board of cultivated fields with scattered square houses for pieces."

It was a matter of regret to us that we had not the time to visit Tassi-chu Jong, for in some respects it must be one of the most interesting places in Bhutan. It was built by the first Dharma Raja, who also founded the Lho-drukpa sect of Buddhism, which has remained the distinctive sect of Bhutan. The correct transliteration of the vernacular name—Bhrashis-chhos-rdzong, meaning "the fortress of auspicious doctrine"—is, according to Dr. Graham Sandberg, Tashichhoidzong; but here again I have preferred simplicity to pedantry and have employed the spelling which, so far as I can judge, is phonetically correct.

A climb of between two and three thousand feet through forest of spruce and larch, and later of silver fir, brought us to the summit of the Chiu-li La at 12,900 feet. Away to the right of the track could be seen a number of buildings clinging to the face of a steep cliff. These, we were told, were the nunnery of Kyila, at times a populous resort but at the moment tenanted by only five or six nuns and less than a dozen monks. We made our way to the top of the highest peak in the range, where, on a needle point a thousand feet above the pass, we found a square stone building containing two small rooms—the cell, in all probability, of some wandering hermit. Here we were at the centre of an immense panorama. To the west in the far distance Kanchenjunga and the great cluster of peaks grouped round it like satellites—Kabru, the Dome and Forked Peak, Pandim and Jubonu—rose up beyond a vast tangled maze of mountains filling in the middle distance. Farther north in the middle distance could be picked out the track which we had travelled over from the summit of the Tremo La, and we had no difficulty in following our route as it wound past the peak of Cho-tra-ké, along the banks of the Pa-chu, past Duggye Jong to Paro. Away to the north across the upper valley of the Pa-chu, Cho-mo-lhari stood up like a sentinel on the Tibetan marches, and farther east in the far distance the horizon was cut by a vast range of snow-clad giants, some little-known range in Tibet lying to the north of the land of Twang. South of us in the foreground was a deep and sombre chasm, the valley of the Ha-chu, and on the far side of it a long dusky ridge, almost the last great range lying between us and the Bengal Duars.

Ha Jong, the ancestral home of the Deb Zimpon, Tobgay Dorjé, and the last of the great baronial castles which we were to see, is a substantial square building on the right bank of the Ha-chu, at an altitude of rather over 9000 feet. It is of recent construction, having been completed by Uggyen Raja in 1915, a year or so before his death, the old jong at Tumphiong, half a mile lower down the river, having become unsafe with age. Our host told us that it had taken two or three years in the building. Its lay-out is simple, a large square keep in the centre of a square courtyard formed by the inner walls of the surrounding building.

Tobgay Dorjé, who succeeded Uggyen Raja as Bhutanese agent on the latter's death, is destined to play a great part in the future of his country. Until quite recently he must have been the only Western-educated man in Bhutan. He had the inestimable advantage of being brought up at Kalimpong with Dr. Graham's own children, and was educated later at St. Paul's School, Darjeeling. As Bhutanese Agent he resides during the summer months at Ha, and during the remainder of the year at Kalimpong, all official correspondence between the Bhutanese Government and the Government of India passing through his hands. With the enthusiastic support of His Highness the Maharaja, and with the cordial advice and co-operation of Drs. Graham and Sutherland, he has organised a school, where some forty boys from Bhutan are being given a modern education up to the university matriculation standard. It is the hope of the Maharaja that these boys may obtain a training in various professions such as medicine, teaching, engineering, and so on, in educational institutions in British India, and may then return to Bhutan to form the nuclei of training establishments in their own country. What this would mean to the future of the country it is easy to foresee. And while it would give a great impetus to the development of Bhutan, it could not but increase the intercourse with, and the friendly relations between, this picturesque mountain state and its powerful neighbour.

The walls of the Ha valley are high and steep and the sun sinks behind them early—about 3.30 P.M. at this season. The air is cold in consequence, and we registered twelve degrees of frost at night. We set forth on the last stage of our journey on November the 5th, and doing short marches made Chamurchi Duar, one of the famous natural gateways on to the plains, on the seventh day. The greater part of the route we followed was said never before to have been traversed by a European. It provided little of interest, however, climbing up and down heavily wooded mountain sides sparsely peopled for the first few days, but colonised by Nepalis as we got nearer to the plains. The ascent from the Ha valley led over the range by a pass of 11,800 feet called the Se-li La, which we crossed on the second day. On the fifth day we dropped to the Amo-chu, which we crossed at an altitude of about 2000 feet. It was the upper waters of this river that we had followed on our journey up the Chumbi valley from Yatung to the vicinity of Phari, tracking it to its source at the foot of Cho-mo-lhari. Its waters, after it leaves the mountains and flows through the Bengal Duars, were likewise familiar to me under the name of the Torsa. It seems more than likely that a comparatively easy route from the plains up to Chumbi might be found along its banks, as was suggested by Captain (now Colonel) O'Connor some years ago.

The last pass between us and the plains, the Yebo La, was crossed on November the 10th, the sixth day out from Ha, and we camped that night a mile or two beyond the crest on a wooded spur, from which we gazed over the far-stretching plains of Bengal into the warm haze which blurs the horizon. Chamurchi Duar is worthy of its name. It is, indeed, a fine natural gateway—a narrow defile between walls of rock green with creepers, through which a mountain stream forces its way. Once through this we found ourselves amid the familiar surroundings of the plains once more. The sun blazed down with its accustomed warmth; the ground, where it was not cultivated, was covered with masses of sweet-smelling wild thyme; long lines of prim-looking tea bushes lay side by side in prosaic regularity upon the face of the land; and away on the plain, some miles from the foot of the mountains, the smoke of a railway train rose lazily from the little station of Bannarhat.

CHAPTER XXIII

THE OUTSTANDING GLORY OF BUDDHISM

THE story of my wanderings in the Eastern Himalayas has now been told; and I have but a few words to add upon an aspect of Buddhism of which little has been said in the preceding pages—that is, the silent and, perhaps, scarcely recognised influence which the teaching of Gautama has exercised upon the conduct of mankind.

From what has already been written it should be clear that the Thera Vada represents the teaching of Buddha as being strictly limited, not by his own knowledge—for having obtained perfect enlightenment he was omniscient—but by what he considered to be expedient in the interests of those whom he taught. Over and over again he is represented as emphasising as the cardinal fact for man, that all earthly existence is sorrow, and that since this is so, it behoves mankind to concentrate its whole energies upon freeing itself from existence. "And what, O disciples, have I preached unto you? 'This is suffering'—thus, O disciples, have I proclaimed unto you. 'This is the origin of suffering'—thus have I proclaimed unto you. 'This is the cessation of suffering'—thus have I proclaimed unto you."[1] It did not profit a man to speculate on what, if anything, lay beyond this life of sorrow. Sufficient unto the day was the evil thereof, and the task of escaping from this vale of tears was one which was only within the compass of man, if he devoted himself exclusively to its accomplishment.

This being so, Gautama was perfectly logical in acquiescing in the ideas which were prevalent with regard to the structure of the universe, for questions of cosmogony had no particular bearing one way or the other, upon the lesson which he sought to impart. The existence of the heavens and the gods of popular belief was immaterial, so long as it was not claimed for them that they were exempt from the universal law of causation. The heavens in this view were mere glorified worlds and the gods mere super-men. Their lives might be of greater duration and more glorious in all respects than those of men; but they, like men, were within, and not without, the ceaseless cycle of becoming, and were borne along as inexorably upon the unending stream of change.

The adherents of the Thera Vada were content to accept this position, and, while affirming the omniscience of Buddha, did not question his wisdom in laying down limits to the knowledge which he imparted to men. "What think ye, my disciples," he is reported to have asked on one occasion when residing in the Sinsapa grove at Kosamba, "whether are more these few Sinsapa leaves which I have gathered in my hand, or

[1] *Buddha*, by H. Oldenberg.

the other leaves yonder in the Sinsapa grove ?" And on receiving the answer he is represented as saying: "So also, my disciples, is that much more which I have learned and have not told you than that which I have told you."[1]

It necessarily followed from the doctrine as set forth in the Thera Vada that a man must rely entirely upon himself for escape from that which was represented as being a state of continuous suffering, namely, life on earth or in any of the other worlds, heavenly or the reverse, which were included in the cosmography of the day. Emphasis is perpetually laid upon this. "Therefore, O Ananda, be ye lamps unto yourselves. Be ye a refuge to yourselves. Betake yourselves to no external refuge. Hold fast to the Truth as a lamp. Hold fast as a refuge to the Truth. Look not for refuge to any one besides yourselves."[2] And after foretelling on one occasion his own approaching end, Gautama is reported to have said: "My age is now full ripe, my life draws to its close: I leave you, I depart, relying on myself alone."[3] With no Saviour to whom to appeal for help; with no promise of a reward hereafter beyond a cessation of existence as known to human experience, which, despite the dictum that it was an unmixed evil human nature insisted upon regarding as desirable, the doctrine was scarcely likely to make any strong appeal to the average man. It was calculated rather to chill any but the most stalwart rationalist who

[1] *Buddha*, by H. Oldenberg.

[2] *The Book of the Great Decease*, translated by T. W. and C. A. F. Rhys Davids.

[3] *Ibid.*

had succeeded in atrophying his emotional nature, and exalting his intellect to such a pitch as to crush out of existence all characteristics except an unchallenged self-reliance. Gautama himself had no illusions as to this.

"Into the mind of the Exalted One," we are told, "came this thought; I have penetrated this deep truth which is difficult to perceive, and difficult to understand, peace-giving, sublime, which transcends all thought, deeply significant, which only the wise can grasp. . . . For man it will be very difficult to grasp this matter, the law of causality, the chain of causes and effects: and this also will be very difficult for him to grasp, the extinction of all conformations, the withdrawal from all that is earthly, the extinction of desire, the cessation of longing, the end, the Nirvana."[1]

And when, as we read in the Great Discourse on Causation, Ananda declared that the doctrine seemed to him to be perfectly clear, Gautama rebuked him saying—"Say not so, Ananda, say not so! Deep is this doctrine of events as arising from Causes. It is through not understanding this doctrine, through not penetrating it, that this generation has become a tangled skein, a matted ball of thread, like to munja-grass and rushes, unable to pass over the doom of the waste, the woeful way, the downfall, the constant round of transmigration."[2]

Whatever place, then, may be accorded to the

[1] *Buddha*, by H. Oldenberg.

[2] *The Maha-Nidana Suttanta*, translated by T. W. and C. A. F. Rhys Davids.

great doctrines of impermanence (" becoming ") and causation among the achievements of the human intellect, it cannot be said of them that they are of a kind to prove attractive to the ordinary man. Hence, as has been shown, the rise of the Mahayānist school. But if the pure doctrine of the Thera Vada lacked the elements of popularity, the phase of thought represented by later developments in Mahayāna Buddhism lacked the elements of permanence, as was proved by its decay and final disappearance from the plains of India. If, then, it is neither the logic of the Thera Vada nor the mysticism and thearchy of the Mahayāna that have proved to be the living glories in Buddhism, what is it in the teaching of Gautama, that has left so abiding an impress upon the world? For no one who has sought to enter into the thought of Eastern lands can doubt the existence of such an impress. For my own part I have little hesitation in ascribing the great influence which the life and teaching of Gautama, have exercised upon the world, to the lofty ethical content of his commandments to mankind. As I have already pointed out, it was not in the selfish, if passionless, abstention from the duties and responsibilities of life, so popular among the teachers of his day, that Gautama found the answer which he sought. It was in the last of the four Noble Truths that he found the solution of his problem—in the pursuit of the Noble Eightfold Path—Right Faith, Right Resolve, Right Speech, Right Action, Right Living, Right Effort, Right Thought, Right Self-concentration. This was the famous

Middle Way giving egress from the iron cage, within whose prison bars revolved inexorably and unendingly the pitiless cycle of existence, ringing the changes from birth to old age, from old age to death, and from death to birth again.

Neither along the road of worldly pleasure nor along the gloomy pathway of self-mortification was salvation to be found, but along the way of duty. In the Noble Eightfold Path we find the positive expression of a code of conduct of which the table of the Mosaic law gives us a more negative definition. In essence they are one and the same—the living by man of his life, involving the performance of his daily task, in accordance with a standard of conduct which is characterised as right.

I am well aware of the difficulties of laying down any absolute standard of right. What may be thought right in one set of circumstances or at one time, may be thought wrong in other circumstances or at another time. Who is to decide? In the case of the Noble Eightfold Path—Right Faith, Right Resolve, Right Speech, and so on—who is to be the arbiter of what constitutes Right? For the man who puzzles himself with such questions the answer implied in Buddhism is given more categorically in the *Bhagavad Gita*, wherein it is definitely stated that man winneth not freedom from action by abstaining from activity, nor by mere renunciation does he rise to perfection; "but he whose works are all free from the moulding of *desire*; he who having abandoned attachment to the fruit of action; hoping for naught, his mind and self controlled, having abandoned all greed, performing action by the body alone, he doth not commit Sin." In more recent times a philosopher of the West has asked a similar question and has given a similar answer. In his view it was the distinguishing mark of a morally good action that it was done not because it was pleasant to the doer, nor because it conduced to his profit in any way, but only because it was right in obedience to what he called a "categorical imperative," that is, to a law which commands not hypothetically—"if you would avoid this," "if you would have that"—but *unconditionally*.[1] The *Bhagavad Gita*, however, was composed many centuries before the days of Kant; and it is this ideal of lofty altruism, this idea of complete selflessness, this sublime indifference to the fruits of works, which, running like golden threads through the ethical teaching of Buddhism and repeated over and over again in the "Song of the Lord," is one of the outstanding glories of Indian thought.

It is not, however, with questions of this kind that the masses puzzled their heads. For them the simple injunctions of a loving heart were all-sufficient. And for all its abstruse doctrines Buddhism showed a comprehensive understanding of the psychology of the ordinary man. It gathered together the folklore which was current in its day—the most complete and the most ancient collection of folklore, in the opinion of

[1] The philosopher, of course, was Kant. I have quoted almost verbatim from Mr. C. C. Y. Webb's *History of Philosophy* the above explanation of Kant's "categorical imperative."

Professor Rhys Davids, now extant in any literature in the world—and m ulding the fables to suit its purpose, produced a collection under the title of the Jataka stories, which provided the masses with a series of lessons in moral conduct admirably suited to their intellectual compass. And it was the custom of Gautama himself to prepare the way for the exposition of the more abstruse doctrine by a disquisition on the nature of an upright life—a rehearsal of the virtues which it behoved a man to practise in every transaction of his daily round. A man was to cultivate "good will without measure towards the whole world, above, below, around, unstinted, unmixed with any feeling of differing or opposing interests."

It was this spirit of loving-kindness that touched the heart of the Emperor Asoka, with incalculable results to the history of the Eastern world. This great scion of the Maurya dynasty came to the throne of a vast empire in the year 272 B.C.; and for the first twelve years of his reign lived riotously, in all probability, amid surroundings of pomp and luxury common to the courts of those days. In the year 261 B.C., with a view to adding to his already extensive dominions, he embarked upon an expedition against the kingdom of Kalinga lying on the coast of the Bay of Bengal and embracing territory now included in the provinces of Madras and Orissa. Conquest was achieved, but not before 150,000 of the people of Kalinga had been carried into captivity, 100,000 slain, and many more had perished as an indirect result of the war.

It was remorse at the contemplation of these fruits of imperial ambition that turned the heart of Asoka towards the kindly teaching of Buddha. And henceforth he pursued the path of *ahiṁsa* with a zeal which secured for him a reputation as the greatest missionary that the world has seen. He sent forth teachers to preach the gospel of loving-kindness to three continents—Western Asia, Eastern Europe, and North Africa. And he spread the doctrine broadcast over India and Ceylon. His revulsion against the shedding of blood was marked in a dramatic manner. The royal hunt which had played so prominent a part among the pastimes of the Court was suppressed; the slaying of animals for sacrifice was forbidden; the daily slaughter for the royal kitchens, referred to by Asoka himself in the first of his famous rock edicts, was brought to an end and the Emperor became a vegetarian.

Not only did he bring to universal notice the law of piety and, in general, the right conduct of man based on the broad foundation of *ahiṁsa*, by means of edicts graven upon rock in widely separated parts of the country and inscribed upon pillars set up in the busy haunts of men; but he laid it down that it was part of the normal duty of his officers of all ranks to teach and enforce the law of duty. And later he took the further step of appointing special officers of high rank entitled Dharma-mahamatras, with a staff of assistants named Dharma-yuktas, whose sole task it was to compel obedience to the code of conduct formulated in the edicts.

It has been said of him that he found Buddhism an Indian sect and that he made of it a world religion.[1] He did so not by dwelling upon its philosophy or its theology, but by devoting himself exclusively to its ethics. As Professor Rhys Davids has pointed out, there is throughout the edicts no word either of God or of the soul. His law of piety is a code of conduct pure and simple. It is the influence of such teaching which impresses itself upon the traveller in Buddhist lands and which displays itself in a certain atmosphere of gentleness and kindness in which the people live. The keynote of human relationships in such lands does, indeed, seem to be the word *ahiṁsa*, rendered inadequately enough by the negative word "harmlessness," in that it carries with it the more positive attitude of mind suggested by the word "loving-kindness."

It is, in truth, a golden word before which all the crude and fierce emotions, the elemental and barbarous passions of man—anger, hatred, malice, and all uncharitableness—flee, ashamed. It is permeated with the spirit of the lofty ethic of the *Dhammapada*—"the Path of Right"—wherein it is taught that "enmity never comes to an end through enmity here below; it comes to an end by non-enmity; this has been the rule from all eternity." A rule of conduct at once so simple of understanding, so lofty in ideal, and so pregnant with happiness for man, takes its place, without question, side by side with

[1] By Dr. J. M. Macphail in his excellent monograph entitled *Asoka*, in the Heritage of India Series. I am indebted to the same source for the main facts on which I have based the brief outline of Asoka given above.

the sublime precepts of Him of Nazareth who commanded men that they should love their enemies, bless them that curse them, do good to them that hate them, and pray for them that despitefully use them and persecute them ; and who proclaimed, " Blessed are the peacemakers, for they shall be called the children of God."

INDEX

THE END

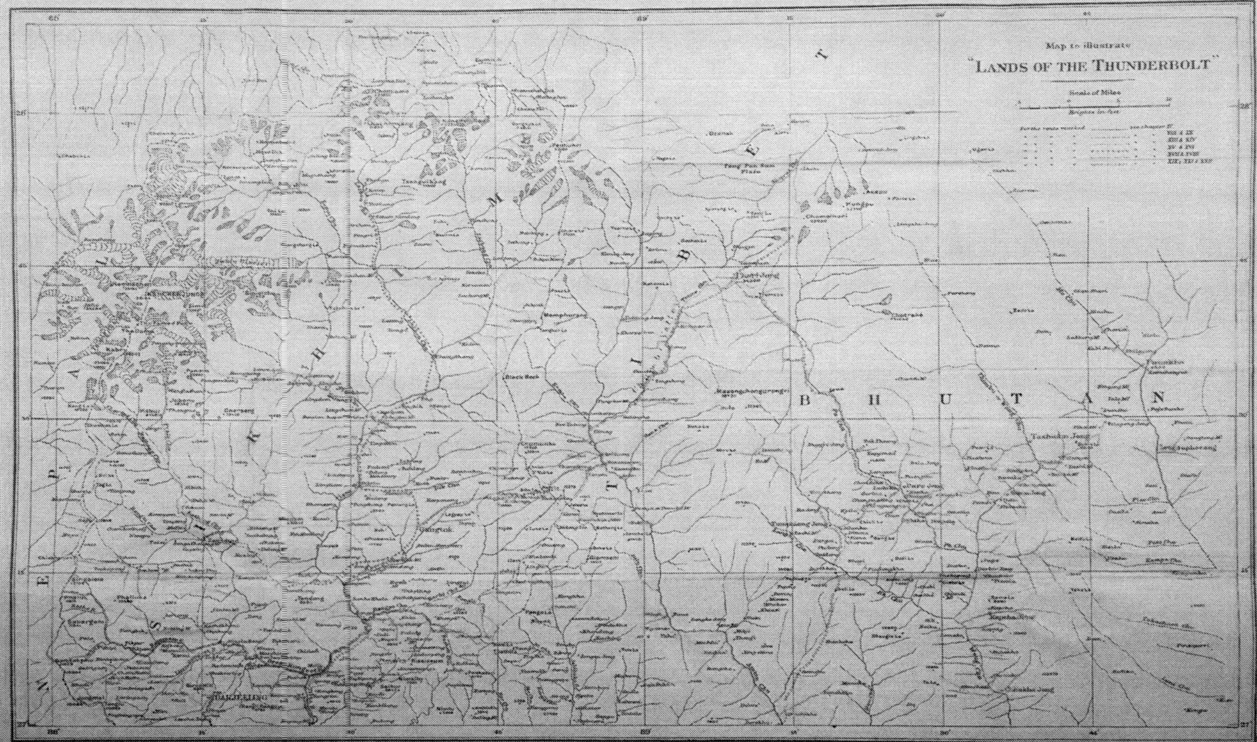
Map to illustrate
"LANDS OF THE THUNDERBOLT"
Scale of Miles
TIBET
SIKHIM
NEPAL
BHUTAN
DARJEELING